for John Shattuck —

with admiration

and warm regards —

Norman Dorsen

July 1988

Southern Illinois University Press

Carbondale and Edwardsville

THE CONSTITUTION, THE LAW, AND FREEDOM OF EXPRESSION

1787–1987

Edited by
James Brewer Stewart

Foreword by
The Honorable
Warren E. Burger

Library of Congress Cataloging-in-Publication Data

The Constitution, the law, and freedom of expression,
   1787–1987.

   Contributions to the 1st Wallace Conference on "the
Constitution, Freedom of Expression, and the Liberal
Arts," held in Sept. 1986 at Macalester College; sponsored
by the college.
   1. Freedom of speech—United States—History—
Congresses.   2. Freedom of the press—United States—
History—Congresses.   I. Stewart, James Brewer.
II. Burger, Warren E., 1907–   .   III. Wallace
Conference on "the Constitution, Freedom of Expression,
and the Liberal Arts" (1st:1986:Macalester College)
IV. Macalester College.
KF4770.A75C67   1987   342.73'0853   87-13106
ISBN 0-8093-1428-2   347.302853

The paper used in this publication meets the minimum
requirements of American National Standard for
Information Sciences—Permanence of Paper for Printed
Library Materials,   ANSI Z 39.48-1984. ∞™

CONTENTS

PREFACE

The 1986 Wallace Conference on "The Constitution, Freedom of Expression, and the Liberal Arts" exemplifies Macalester College's commitment to free, uninhibited inquiry and expression, within a legal tradition that protects the rights of the individual and provides for the welfare of the greater society. The flourishing of education in this country, from the natural and social sciences to the humanities and fine arts, is due in large part to the support provided by the Constitution and the way of life it makes possible.

It could not have been more appropriate for the first Wallace Conference to be held during the time the nation was beginning its celebration of the bicentennial of the Constitution, the basic document of governance that has provided freedom and democracy to our nation for almost two centuries. No other form of government has been as successful as ours in protecting basic freedoms and no other receives as much critical attention.

The freedom to praise or criticize all aspects of our lives, including the very document that supports those freedoms, is precious. Those who participated in this conference are excellent examples of the theme and the tradition.

Macalester College, in the tradition of liberal arts colleges, seeks to educate persons who will become good citizens and leaders in American society. We believe that the best way to accomplish this is to bring together a talented group of students to be educated by a faculty of dedicated teacher-scholars with a broadly based program deeply rooted in the arts, humanities, and sciences. In addition, we are convinced that both students and faculty need constant challenges from those seminal minds who are shaping the various disciplines—and our society as a whole. The Wallace Visitors Program, with its emphasis on bringing outstanding scholars to the Macalester campus and giving our students and faculty the opportunity to interact with them, is an example of what we do best.

We were honored that the Bicentennial Commission designated the Wallace Conference as an official bicentennial event.
The essays that follow are in accord with the finest traditions of
both the college and the nation.

Robert M. Gavin, Jr.
President
Macalester College

FOREWORD

Warren E. Burger

Apart from honoring the memory and work of DeWitt Wallace, the conference in which the following essays originated had two objectives, both involving anniversaries. On the one hand, the Wallace Conference celebrated the one-hundredth anniversary of Macalester College as among America's small but great liberal arts colleges. On the other hand, it saluted the two-hundredth anniversary of history's greatest example of basic organic law, the Constitution of the United States.

At the beginning of our activities, we on the national Commission on the Bicentennial of the United States Constitution took as our mission to give ourselves and the American people a history and civics lesson about that document. We need to know more about how it came to be written and ratified and what it has meant to us. We also must assess and appreciate its continuing and pervasive impact on our own lives and, indeed, on the lives of people all over the world.

Because of the basic integrity of the document itself, the Constitution has stood the test of time. At its inception, it embodied the ideas of the best thinkers of earlier periods and a special, daring genius. Its framing and ratification marked an unparalleled advance in human freedom and the art of government. In our own time, no less than in 1787, the strength to secure freedom involves risks as well as rewards, and, indeed, the risks themselves are what make the rewards possible.

The men who created the Constitution certainly knew as much about risks as about rewards when they set about their work. When Hamilton, Madison, and others, with Washington's silent but powerful assent, initially attempted to move forward with the creation of a new central government, they faced thirteen independent sovereigns that called themselves "states" in the fullest sense of the term. State leaders were jealous of their independence; they looked with hostility on any diminution of their sovereignty. The Articles of Confederation contained a provision guaranteeing that "each state retains its sovereignty, freedom

ix

and independence" and the states had done no more than agreed "to enter into a firm league of friendship" with each other. That is the language generally used in multilateral treaties between truly sovereign states for limited and particular purposes. France, Germany, and Italy might approach each other on such terms today to negotiate trade agreements. Little wonder, then, that in 1786, when Madison, Hamilton, and their supporters in Annapolis convened what was ostensibly a gathering on commercial matters but soon moved to a discussion of a new, stronger central government, only five states took enough interest to send representatives. Even the host state, Maryland, was not represented.

And when the same single-minded leaders next tried to secure approval from the Continental Congress for the Constitutional Convention, they encountered opposition from all quarters. The most Hamilton and Madison could secure was a resolution that delegates should be sent to Philadelphia for "the sole and express purpose" of revising the Articles of Confederation, *not* for the purpose of writing a new constitution. Under such constraints only the most venturesome of "risk takers" would have continued to pursue the idea of totally transforming the framework of government for thirteen such fractious states. But of course, that is exactly what they did.

And the risks hardly stopped here. Common people were no less jealous of their local independence than most of the leaders. It would require much persuasion to convince them that their freedom would be more firmly secured, not crushed, by the new central government that Madison, Hamilton, and Washington envisioned. When, for example, some new recruits from New Jersey reported to Washington at Valley Forge, they refused to swear allegiance to the United States, saying "our country is New Jersey." For much the same reason, Washington watched his army dissolve whenever he marched it across a state boundary line. Soldiers would gladly fight for their own states but loyalty to others was limited.

In light of such widespread attitudes, we can surely sympathize with Madison, who wrote, after the delegates finished their work in Philadelphia, "The real wonder is that so many difficulties should have been surmounted, and surmounted with a unanimity almost as unprecedented as it must have been expected. It is impossible for the man of pious reflection not to perceive [in this circumstance] a finger of that Almighty hand which has been so frequently and signally extended to our relief in the critical stages of the revolution."[1]

Franklin, not much noted for his piety, must have shared Madison's feeling that the problems of drafting a new constitution were so formidable as to require divine intervention. When the delegates convened in Philadelphia, Franklin suggested that every meeting open with a prayer as was done in the Continental Congress.

That the Founding Fathers struggled against great adversity to get their document drafted and ratified is a matter of public record. Patrick Henry, one of Virginia's most powerful politicians, was designated as a delegate to the Philadelphia Convention, but declined, saying, "Me thinks I smell a rat." The "rat," of course, was the stronger central government he feared so greatly. Of more than seventy designated delegates, at least fifteen chose to emulate Henry, and Rhode Island refused even to select delegates. The real work of the Convention fell to about forty-five of those who attended regularly. The greatest risk they ran, of course, was that their work would be rejected, that the states would refuse to agree to so significant a diminution of state power. Such a result was precisely what some members of the Continental Congress aimed for when they first reviewed the proposed Constitution. A resolution was offered criticizing the delegates to Philadelphia for having exceeded their authority.

But to the Founding Fathers, the potential rewards were self-evident and clearly built into the risks. The rewards included the prospect of a truly national government, capable of expanding liberty on a national scale, structured to encourage manufacture, trade, commerce, and orderly growth for the country as a whole. The possibility of defeating parochial attitudes also offered the glowing prospect of creating a truly national and liberating republican government.

John Dickinson captured both the anxiety and the anticipation of the Founders' situation when he wrote, "If the [national] government should be left dependent on the State Legislatures, it would be happy for us if we never meet in this room." So did another delegate, Nicholas Gilman, who wrote to his wife, "[The creation of this Constitution] was done by bargain and compromise. Yet notwithstanding its imperfections, on the adoption of it depends . . . whether we shall become a respectable nation or a people torn to pieces by intestine commotions."[2]

These two hundred years bear witness to what that delegate had to say about "intestine commotions." The American Civil War and two devastating and debilitating world wars only begin the tragic list that regional and international rivalries have brought about. Yet throughout these travails, the Constitution has endured and our country has grown stronger. That it has done so is, in itself, an enormous tribute to the remarkable leadership of that small group of men who met in Philadelphia.

But the Constitution's endurance also raises a disturbing thought—what if it had not been ratified? What if America had not finally been persuaded by the same logic that prompted Ben Franklin's closing remarks at the end of the Philadelphia Convention? Franklin declared, "I confess there are several parts of this constitution which I do not at present approve, but I am not sure I will ever approve them. For having lived long, I have experienced many instances of being obliged by better information and fuller consideration to change opinions even on very important subjects, which I once thought right, but found to be otherwise. In these sentiments, sir, I agree to this constitution with all its faults, if they are such."[3]

What if too few Americans had shared Franklin's view and the Constitution had been defeated? We must shudder to think of the consequences if large states like New York and Virginia had held back. Even though nine states had already ratified the Constitution before Virginia approved it by the scant margin of eighty-nine votes to seventy-nine, a rejection at that stage might have led to the kind of "intestine commotion" that would have delayed our nation's unique development as a free people and a prosperous republic.

We can only speculate on these hazards that were avoided, since the happy fact is that the risks did prove to be worth taking in the time of the Founding Fathers. They remain so in ours. President Grover Cleveland remarked at the one-hundredth anniversary of the Constitution, "If the American people are true to their sacred trust, another centennial day will come, and millions yet unborn will inquire concerning our stewardship and the safety of their Constitution. God grant they may find it unimpaired."[4] That day is nearly upon us. Let us remember as we ponder the following essays that millions yet unborn will inquire concerning our stewardship of their Constitution, just as we have of those who have gone before us. God grant that they may find it unimpaired.

NOTES

1. James Madison, "The Federalist No. 37," in *The Federalist*, ed. Jacob E. Cooke (Middletown, Conn.: Wesleyan Univ. Press, 1961), p. 238.

2. Dickinson quoted in Catherine Drinker Bowen, *Miracle at Philadelphia: The Story of the Constitutional Convention, May to September 1787* (Boston: Little, Brown–Atlantic Monthly Press, 1966), p. 185; Nicholas Gilman, letter to Joseph Gilman, 18 Sept. 1787, in *The Records of the Federal Convention of 1787*, ed. Max Farrand, rev. ed. in 4 vols. (New Haven: Yale Univ. Press, 1937), 3:82.

3. Franklin quoted in *Records of the Federal Convention of 1787*, ed. Farrand, 2:641–42.

4. Cleveland quoted in *The One-Hundredth Anniversary of the Constitution of the United States*, ed. H. L. Carson (Philadelphia: J. B. Lippincott, 1889), 2:262.

THE CONSTITUTION, THE LAW, AND FREEDOM OF EXPRESSION

1787–1987

INTRODUCTION

James Brewer Stewart

> The community that will not protect its most ignorant and un-
> popular member in the free utterance of his opinions, no matter
> how false or hateful, is only a gang of slaves.
>
> Wendell Phillips
> "The Scholar in the Republic"

This, to Wendell Phillips, the preeminent libertarian, abolition-
ist, and orator of the Civil War era, was the inevitable cost of cur-
tailing freedom of expression. The victimizers themselves also
became victims, and democratic culture was degraded on all levels. Conversely, he believed, the greater the range of public discussion, the healthier the condition of American liberty. In his
view, the highest duty of the scholar was simply to enrich the
debate, "to entertain no object but truth, to tear a question open
and riddle it with light." The contributors of essays to this volume, extraordinarily diverse in their accomplishments and perspectives, illustrate the truth of Phillips's assertions. This is
largely because each is (as was Phillips) an activist, as well as a
scholar, to whom the practice of free expression is personally
and professionally essential.

The nature of the conference in which these contributors participated and in which these essays had their origin gives support to Phillips's opinion. Sponsored by Macalester College in
September 1986 and entitled "The Constitution, Freedom of Expression, and the Liberal Arts," the conference was designed
specifically to enrich the right of freedom of expression and the
general public's understanding of that right by encouraging its
freest practice. Those addressing the conference were selected
not only for their scholarly eminence, but also for their power to
activate public discourse through the powerful expression of
their ideas and values. All participants agreed to address the

1

conference theme in relation to some contemporary topic with which they feel deeply involved.

Three of the contributing essayists are practitioners of the law. Warren E. Burger, recently retired as chief justice from our highest judicial body, has refocused his activism from law *per se* to directing the work of the national Commission on the Bicentennial of the United States Constitution. Antonin Scalia and Norman Dorsen continue to make their distinguished careers synonymous with legal disputation on the highest levels —especially in the Supreme Court of the United States. There Scalia sits as associate justice. There also, Dorsen, president of the American Civil Liberties Union, has often argued cases with national significance, many involving First Amendment rights.

In their essays all three men place high premium on the fundamental importance of law and its historical development as the bedrock of individual freedom in America. Equitable laws and illuminating precedents, they argue, are what we must rely upon most of all to preserve and extend our rights of self-expression. To be sure, these three essays address a widely dissimilar set of subjects. Still, a basic reliance on law and history to secure personal liberties underlies them all.

Warren Burger, as we have seen, meditates intensely on the daring of the Founding Fathers, who, he suggests, fashioned a Constitution that has not only endured, but that has also established a tradition that gives Americans of every generation the opportunity to enjoy a fuller measure of freedom than did its predecessors. "An unparalleled advance in human freedom and the art of government" in its own day, the Constitution was born, Burger emphasizes, through the efforts of "risk takers." The Founding Fathers, he reminds us, worked against powerful forces of parochialism, risking not only the failure of their own efforts but also the political fragmentation of the new nation in order to insure our "unique development as a free people and a prosperous republic." Today, Burger concludes, Americans must become cognizant of this tradition by studying the Constitution and its history. By these means, American citizens can remain able to take intelligent risks of their own on behalf of freedom of expression in a threatening, rapidly changing world. In the absence of such historical consciousness, Burger feels, freedom of expression faces bleak prospects.

Antonin Scalia locates the sources of free expression in precise legal reasoning, as well as in important historical developments. He emphasizes that "the law displays enormous evolution over the past fifty years" in First Amendment cases, especially since the era of World War I. Then, restrictions on free expression abounded on the state level because such matters were not considered to be legitimate concerns of the federal courts. Today, however, the Fourteenth Amendment has been interpreted to extend the guarantees of the First Amendment to the state level. Protections of freedom of expression of all sorts have expanded greatly, thanks in part to the impact of new technologies in expanding opportunities for articulating such expression. But, Scalia emphasizes, this proliferation of freedom has also forced courts to make essential distinctions between various *types* of expression, some of which have been accorded greater legal protection than others. As "speech" of all sorts has become freer, Scalia demonstrates, guarantees of protection for various categories of "speech" have necessarily become less equal. With impressive precision, he explains the sources of this seeming paradox, showing how jurists have developed such distinctions and why such distinctions are essential for the maintenance of "freedom of expression" in its wider sense.

At first reading, Norman Dorsen's views on freedom of expression seem greatly at odds with both Burger's and Scalia's. Unlike the former, Dorsen sees no evident historical progression towards a freer and stronger nation. Instead, he warns, some of the gravest threats to our liberty stem from the augmenting power of government. Unlike the latter, Dorsen wishes to draw no precise distinction between various forms of expression, some of which enjoy greater protection than others. Instead, he fears for the future of freedom of expression in its entirety, warning of a host of new dangers: new surveillance technologies, new expressions of religious intolerance, new assertions of nationalistic ideology, new forms of discrimination, and new efforts to censor artistic expression.

Yet to preserve American liberty, Dorsen, like Scalia and Burger, emphasizes the profound value of the American law and the historical traditions supporting it. In calling for "a new enlightenment," a reassertion of the eighteenth-century libertarian values that first introduced into Western culture a high regard for the sanctity of individual opinion, he, like Burger, evokes the Founding Fathers. In demanding the application of enlightened legal reasoning to insure the maximum feasible protection of all expression, he parallels Scalia's methods. In this respect, these three essays offer fascinatingly diverse, yet clearly related, legal perspectives on freedom of expression, its prospects, and its place in American law.

The remaining contributors to this collection regard freedom of expression in ways that depart markedly from their legal colleagues. Mary Beth Norton's prize-winning feminist scholarship has helped revolutionize our understanding of America's past and of women's roles in shaping our history. Through his award-winning writings, Robert Jay Lifton, psychiatrist and social psychologist, has fundamentally challenged conventional wisdom on the meanings of nuclear weapons and modern totalitarianism. Harry B. Gray's brilliant discoveries in inorganic chemistry have led us closer to scientific answers to the staggering problems of hunger, pollution, and shrinking sources of energy. John Edgar Wideman has employed rich literary gifts to powerfully evoke the experiences of Afro-Americans and to explicate the significance these experiences have for all of us. But for all their diversity, these essayists all stress that powerful social forces, often beyond the law, define the limits of free expression.

They also agree that freedom of expression depends more on the transformation of our personal and collective consciousness of these forces than it does on legal guarantees. Mary Beth Norton, for example, reminds us vividly that for much of the nation's history, unwritten gender biases, not formal codes, have played a determining role in restricting women's rights of free expression. Conversely, evolving feminist consciousness and activism, not litigation alone, have most often supported those who have struggled to claim that right. The eighteenth-century Enlightenment, she observes, held out little promise for women. While Locke, Rousseau, and the Founding Fathers expanded male freedom, they systematically defined women as irrelevant to the political community, leaving them no voice in public affairs. For this reason, feminists of that time looked not to the law but to the development of female education as the surest support for achieving the right of self-expression. Forward-thinking activists such as Judith Sargent Murray argued that women must be educated for their own development as individuals, rather than as adornments for their husbands-to-be or in preparation for motherhood. In making these demands, Murray built on feminist thinking with origins in the Renaissance. But more important, as Norton emphasizes, her demand for *individual* self-realization marked a particular new phase of consciousness, prefiguring the generation of feminists that followed her. Led by Susan B. Anthony and Elizabeth Cady Stanton, Murray's successors would make unprecedented demands for full female equality in speech, in politics, and in domestic relations as well.

Robert Jay Lifton, like Norton, finds the essence of free expression in transformations of consciousness, not in interpretations of law. His essay speaks to our deep concern over the possibility of global annihilation by nuclear weapons. But just as dangerous as the weapons themselves, in Lifton's view, is our widely shared psychological incapacity to think, feel, and speak authentically about the threats these weapons pose. We suffer from "suppressed consciousness," Lifton warns; we are inhibited by powerful cultural constraints and political circumstances from developing the ideas necessary for effective self-expression about the nuclear threat. "We become," he writes, "emotionally paralyzed to think clearly in the face of terrifying reality."

The purpose of Lifton's essay is therefore to locate and understand the *sources* of this paralysis, the better to recognize and overcome them. For this reason, he emphasizes the power of various images associated with nuclear weapons and global destruction, such as "nuclear winter," the "winnable" nuclear war, "Star Wars," "survivalism," the Chernobyl disaster, and others. By confronting and analyzing these images, Lifton suggests, one begins to understand the substructures of emotion and cultural conditioning that impede our honest responses to the nuclear threat. And with such understanding, he argues further, we can also develop "a new psychology of human survival," a perspective that can overcome the crippling ambivalence about nuclear weapons that Lifton believes our culture imparts to us.

Harry Gray shares Lifton's concerns about technology's relationship to global problems. And, like Lifton, he fears that public discussion of these relationships is being dangerously distorted by false perceptions and misinformation. Specifically, Gray warns that the news media make it increasingly difficult for citizens to become knowledgeable about developments in science and their impact on the quality of modern life.

There is much in today's scientific research that should command the public's attention, Gray stresses. A "scientific revolution" has overtaken all research fields, including his own of chemistry. Important in their own right, these developments also become particularly newsworthy since they promise significant results in struggle against disease, hunger, pollution, and other worldwide ills. Gray fears, however, that today's media, often more concerned with markets than with accuracy, too often distort the reporting of science. Some scientists, as a result, have become distrustful of the media and reluctant to discuss their work in public. Others have begun to exploit the media to advance their visibility by engaging in "publication by press conference," claiming definitive results that in fact have yet to be proven. In short, Gray warns, the impact of the "scientific revolution" is compounding rapidly. Yet, because of the influence of the media, the public's ability to understand, discuss, and evaluate this revolution is diminishing in proportion.

"Voices not heard are eloquent in their absence . . . their unrecorded *no* breaks through the drone of consensus." From this remark John Edgar Wideman develops a powerful meditation on the nature of free expression that directly addresses all of the other essays collected here. It challenges wholesale the assumptions of Burger, Scalia, and Dorsen, for to Wideman freedom of expression has little to do with the accepted conventions of law, logic, and history. It also amplifies on Norton's, Lifton's, and Gray's equation of free expression with transformed consciousness by developing themes that synthesize all these writers' concerns. The oppression of women, the mystification of nuclear weapons, and the media's distorted reporting of science can all be seen as facets of the larger problem of free expression that Wideman isolates.

Legal structures, Wideman grants, can and do provide crucial barriers against the suppression of speech. Yet, on deeper levels, law also represents an elaborate ritual that we, as a culture, have constructed to mask our awareness of the disorder that actually rules in our world. Though we endow it with the illusion of rationality, law, in Wideman's view, actually licenses the use of power, elevating the privileged and the accepted while suppressing the poor and the rejected. The free speech of some, purchased with the silence of others, is then reified as objective truth, as a right we believe all can enjoy, a right to be defended by logic, law, and history. Yet, beneath this perception, Wideman asserts, remains the source of the most eloquent speech of all, the mute words of those whom the dominant culture can no longer hear.

Some, however, do hear these eloquent silences, Wideman insists: our artists, poets, prophets, seers, and rebels, outsiders who "speak with the gift of tongues." To Wideman, these are the truest practitioners of free expression. Their messages originate outside our accepted cultural categories and help us to lift the veils of illusion that we frequently mistake for objective truth.

Wendell Phillips, a seer and prophet himself, endorsed a view similar to Wideman's when he asserted that the duty of the scholar was "to entertain no object but truth, to tear a question open and riddle it with light." Yet Phillips also held a law degree from Harvard and believed passionately that precise laws and their logical application were essential for preserving liberty. Perhaps his ambivalence will help us to understand our own response as we reflect on the contents of this volume.

It is difficult, on the one hand, to contest the view that freedom of expression is inherent in American law and that it is diminished whenever that law is undermined. But, on the other hand, it is also impossible to believe that law can give us the insight to reshape our culture so that its silent voices can speak, be understood, and be allowed to redefine our culture's self-understanding. That, inarguably, requires transformations of consciousness. Between law and transformation, one suspects, exists a tension that we all must struggle to master if freedom of expression is to remain vital to democratic American culture. The essays comprising this volume provide compelling examples of how our thinking might proceed.

1

A HOUSE WITH MANY MANSIONS

Categories of Speech
Under the First Amendment

Antonin Scalia

What I hope to do in the following remarks is to convey some appreciation of the difficulties that judges confront in applying the First Amendment to the liberal arts—or, for that matter, to any aspect of human endeavor. What I want to focus upon, in particular, is the enormous diversity of expressive conduct with respect to which it must be decided whether First Amendment protection exists, and if it does so, the extent of the protection. Hence the title of my talk, "A House with Many Mansions."

The judge's task in this field is complicated at the outset by the fact that there are few areas of constitutional law in which it is less possible to discern a consistent pattern of decision—or even a consistent analytical approach—dating back to the adoption of the Bill of Rights. The teaching of the First Amendment in law schools generally begins with cases decided after World War I, dealing with attempts under the federal Espionage Act of 1917 to suppress, in one fashion or another, dissent from our involvement in the war—and, more specifically, with Justice Oliver Wendell Holmes's opinion in *Schenk v. United States.*[2] Even beginning with those cases, the law displays an enormous evolution in the last fifty years. But if one looks to the Supreme Court precedent before that era (as David Rabban did in a 1981 article in the *Yale Law Journal*[3]), the contrast is even more startling. Let me describe briefly some of the pre–World War I decisions of the

Supreme Court upholding restrictions on speech. (It had not yet been decided, at the time of these cases, that the Fourteenth Amendment extended the guarantees of the First Amendment against the states; but it had not been decided that it did not, either. The cases in the following list involving state rather than federal action either address free-speech objections under the state constitution's equivalent of the First Amendment, or address on the merits, rather than dismissing as nonexistent, free-speech guarantees under the federal Constitution, or proceed with no apparent awareness of any conceivable free-speech problem. All of those dispositions shed light, I think, on what the Court conceived the guarantees of the First Amendment to be.) The Supreme Court upheld the following:

- A Boston city ordinance prohibiting public addresses on public grounds without a permit from the mayor, who was authorized to withhold it in his unbounded discretion.[4]
- An injunction ordering the American Federation of Labor not to announce that a company was on its "Unfair" or "We don't patronize" lists.[5]
- An Ohio law requiring prior approval of all motion picture films by a board of censors.[6]
- A conviction of criminal contempt for publishing articles and a cartoon criticizing judicial behavior, without opportunity to defend on the basis that the criticism was justified.[7]
- A conviction under a Washington statute making it a misdemeanor to publish material "having a tendency to encourage or incite the commission of any crime, breach of the peace or act of violence, or which shall tend to encourage or advocate disrespect for law or for any court or courts of justice." The conviction was based on an article entitled "The Nude and the Prudes," which encouraged a boycott against those who interfered with nude bathing.[8]
- The deportation of an anarchist under the Alien Immigration Act of 1903, which excluded "anarchists, or persons who believe in or advocate the overthrow by force or violence of the Government." It would make no difference, the Court said, whether this particular anarchist in fact supports violent overthrow, since any alien "who avows himself to be an anarchist, without more," adopts the congressional description equating support of anarchy with support of violence and renders himself deportable.[9]

Without heaping example upon example, suffice it to say that at least one pre-*Schenck* case expresses acceptance of the extraordinary view that the First Amendment made no change in inherited English law, which would mean that it did not even prevent criminal prosecution for seditious libel—that is, for statements, however true, that bring the government into disrepute;[10] that a number of pre-*Schenck* cases state that the First Amendment categorically prohibits nothing except *prior restraints* on speech—that is, the suppression of speech beforehand—and allows *any* sort of speech to be punished after the fact, so long as it has some "tendency" to be harmful to the society;[11] and that in a case decided in 1913 the Brief of the Solicitor General unabashedly (I *assume* unabashedly) argues that Congress could exclude from the mails all newspapers "advocating lotteries, prohibition, anarchy, or a protective tariff if a majority of Congress thought such views against public policy."[12]

The *Yale Law Journal* article to which I am indebted for this collection of cases concludes, without much exaggeration, that "[o]nly a few, isolated opinions before World War One indicated that the First Amendment could be more than a paper guarantee."[13] How far that is from the current law should be apparent even to those who have never read a judicial opinion. Yet it was thought to be the law within the lifetime of many who are still with us today. The principal moral, I suppose, is that the First Amendment is a particularly fragile protection, constantly subject to assault in authoritarian times, and thus constantly in need of zealous defense. But the point of this description for present purposes is that the Supreme Court does not have the benefit of a long and coherent doctrinal development dating back to the Marshall Court.

The words of the First Amendment are that "Congress shall make no law . . . abridging the freedom of speech, or of the press. . . ." It has been established (though that did not occur until 1925) that the Fourteenth Amendment extends the prohibitions of the First Amendment to the states—so that the text now reads, in effect, "*The Government* shall make no law . . . abridging the freedom of speech, or of the press. . . ." I want to explore the difficulties bearing upon the two central questions that this text presents: (1) What elements are included within the terms "speech" and "press"? (2) Does "abridgment of the freedom" mean the same thing with regard to all of those elements?

It should be apparent that the two questions are connected. To the extent that one adopts a very narrow definition of what is meant by "speech and press" (for convenience I will generally use the term *speech* to refer to both), to that extent one can afford to be much more uniform about the permissible degree of, or requisite justifications for, government interference. It is generally agreed, for example, that what might be called "political speech"—the expression of views on matters that are, or could be, the subject of governmental action—is entitled to the highest degree of protection from official interference. If that were the *only* sort of expression entitled to First Amendment protection, we would obviously not have to talk about varying degrees, at least insofar as the subject-matter aspect of the expression is concerned. That was the position taken by Professor Meiklejohn, in his provocative article entitled "The First Amendment Is an Absolute." [14]

Let me begin, then, with the categorization of speech along the lines suggested in this last example—on the basis of subject matter. Most highly protected, as I have said—and for obvious reasons, since its protection is utterly central to the purposes of the First Amendment—is political speech. This is the sort of speech (the advocacy of particular courses of action with regard to the government) to which the famous "clear and present danger" test was originally applied in the post–World War I cases; only a threat of immediate harm could justify its suppression. That it remains the most highly protected today is exemplified by a recent opinion of my court, which held that the Washington subway system could not refuse to accept advertising consisting of a photograph of the president and his cabinet pointing and laughing at a group of poor people. The photograph was a composite, but we held that even if that was not apparent, and the photograph was therefore false and deceptive, it could not be rejected by the administrators on that ground. [15]

But political speech is not, of course, the only subject matter to which First Amendment protection has been extended. As the Supreme Court has said, "[O]ur cases have never suggested that expression about philosophical, social, artistic, economic, literary, or ethical matters—to take a nonexhaustive list of labels—is not entitled to full First Amendment protection." [16] In fact, only one subject matter has clearly been held to be off the scale—obscenity, which the Supreme Court has defined (if not adequately described) as speech which "taken as a whole appeal[s] to the prurient interest in sex, which portray[s] sexual conduct in a patently offensive way, and which, taken as a whole, do[es] not have serious literary, artistic, political, or scientific value." [17] Other than that, all subject matter has been held entitled to some First Amendment protection—even advocacy of criminal conduct, which cannot be proscribed unless it is "directed to inciting or producing imminent lawless action and is likely to incite or produce such action." [18]

The degree of protection is not uniform, however. The nature of, or the required governmental justification for, restriction of speech on several subjects differs from the norm. Several opinions suggest, for example, that speech appealing to the prurient interest in sex but not qualifying as obscenity (presumably because it does not do so in a "patently offensive" way, or because it has "serious literary, artistic, political, or scientific value") may be restricted in ways that other speech may not. [19]

Another subject-matter category of speech that is on the lower, less-protected part of the scale is so-called commercial speech, that is, speech which "does no more than propose a commercial transaction." [20] Such speech (even assuming that it is not fraudulent and that the transaction it proposes is lawful) may be restricted if the government's interest in restriction is substantial, the restrictions directly advance the asserted interest, and the restrictions are no more extensive than necessary to advance the interest. [21] The justification for this lessened protection is that commercial speech is thought to be more easily verifiable, less likely to be deterred by proper regulation, and less central to First Amendment values than other types of speech. [22]

By the way, it was not that long ago that commercial speech was treated as completely unprotected by the First Amendment. [23] And in the bad old days commercial speech was not only unprotected but also defined with a breadth that would have had a severe impact upon the liberal arts if it had endured. In the 1915 Supreme Court opinion I alluded to earlier, upholding Ohio's pre-censorship of motion pictures, the Court said:

> We immediately feel that the argument is wrong or strained which extends the guaranties of free opinion and speech to the multitudinous shows which are advertised on the bill-boards of our cities and towns . . . and which seeks to bring motion pictures and other spectacles into practical and legal similitude to a free press and liberty of opinion.
>
> The judicial sense supporting the common sense of the country is against the contention. . . . [T]he police power is familiarly exercised in granting or withholding licenses for theatrical performances as a means of their regulation. . . .
>
> The exercise of the power upon moving picture exhibitions has been sustained. . . .
>
> . . . It cannot be put out of view that the exhibition of moving pictures is a business pure and simple, originated and conducted for profit, like other spectacles, not to be regarded, nor intended to be regarded by the Ohio constitution, we think, as part of the press of the country or as organs of public opinion.[24]

Imagine the different terrain of the First Amendment if this notion of what constitutes unprotected "commercial speech"—that is, not merely speech designed to sell a product, but speech communicated for profit—had prevailed.

A second way of categorizing speech, other than by its subject matter, is by its truth or falsity. False speech receives reduced protection. This may seem difficult to reconcile (and it is) with the famous Supreme Court dictum that states:

> Under the First Amendment there is no such thing as a false idea. However pernicious an opinion may seem, we depend for its correction not on the conscience of judges and juries but on the competition of other ideas.

That dictum, however, is immediately succeeded by the following:

> But there is no constitutional value in false statements of fact. Neither the intentional lie nor the careless error materially advances society's interest in "uninhibited, robust, and wide-open" debate on public issues.[25]

Drawing the line between constitutionally valuable "opinions" (of which, according to *Gertz*, there is "no such thing" as a false one) and constitutionally worthless "false statements of fact" has been one of the major focuses of libel law ever since. (If you see a clear difference between the two, you are either more perceptive or less perceptive than I.) False and deceptive *commercial* speech is regularly subjected to prohibitions to which truthful commercial speech would be constitutionally immune.[26] Even false and deceptive *political* speech can, in certain circumstances and by proper judicial procedures, be proscribed—for example, as occurred in one case, the use of the letters "REP" in the advertising of a candidate running for office, where they assertedly meant that he was the candidate, not of the Republican party, but of the "Representation for Every Person" party.[27]

Another basis for categorizing speech is according to its speaker. The Supreme Court has said, for example, that "[W]hile members of the military services are entitled to the protections of the First Amendment, 'the different character of the military community and of the military mission requires a different application of those protections.'"[28] It has also said that "The First Amendment rights of minors are not 'co-extensive with those of adults'"[29] and that "[a]lthough government employees do not shed their first amendment rights on assuming public responsibilities, the scope of their right to speak freely is narrower than that of private citizens."[30] It has sometimes been suggested, but thus far has never been accepted, that the institutional press (the "media") has particularly expansive First Amendment rights.[31] One might also consider as categorization by speaker (though it might more accurately be considered categorization by location) the Supreme Court's recent upholding of a restriction upon "vulgar" speech by a high school student at a student assembly[32] or its conclusion that "a prison inmate retains [only] those First Amendment rights that are not inconsistent with his status as a prisoner or with the legitimate penological objectives of the corrections system."[33]

But if speech can be categorized on the basis of the identity of the speaker, it can also be categorized on the basis of the nature of the audience. It is well established, for example, that speech

aimed at or readily available to juveniles may be regulated in circumstances where similar speech aimed at or available to adults
could not.[34] There also appears in the case-law, in various contexts, what the Court has called "the 'captive audience' ratio-
nale,"[35] providing reduced protection for speech to which it is
"impractical for the unwilling viewer or auditor to avoid exposure"[36]—such as, for example, political messages on public
buses or trolleys.[37] Closely related, if not identical, to this is the
reduced protection afforded to messages directed, uninvited, to
individuals in the ultimate retreat of their own homes.[38]

Speech may also be categorized on the basis of where it occurs.
Speech on those portions of state-owned property that are traditional "public fora," such as a municipal theater,[39] is afforded
higher protection than speech on government property not nor-
mally open to speakers, such as a military base,[40] or speech on
private property to which the public has been admitted, such as a
shopping center.[41]

Last but not least in this far from exhaustive catalog, I must
mention the categorization of speech by its mode of expression. I
have saved this for last because it contains some of the greatest
difficulties and best exemplifies the complexity of this undertak-
ing of forming a First Amendment jurisprudence. The Supreme
Court has said that "[e]ach method of communicating ideas is 'a
law unto itself' and that law must reflect the 'differing natures,
values, abuses and dangers' of each method."[42] As Charles de
Gaulle is reputed to have observed when an exasperated subal-
tern exclaimed, with Gallic ferocity, "Death to all fools!": "An am-
bitious program." The simplest classifications consist of different
modes of verbal communication. Communication via soundtruck
roaming the public streets, for example, can be subjected to restrictions not permissible for the human voice unaided.[43] The
Court has forbidden a requirement that newspapers provide individuals whom they attack a right to reply,[44] but has permitted
that and more (namely, a requirement that access be provided
to candidates for public office) for over-the-air television.[45] One
of the issues currently wending its way through the courts is
whether cable television is more like newspapers or like over-the-
air television.

But differences among the various modes of verbal communication are as nothing beside the differences between verbal communication and some other forms of expression. For the First Amendment has, of course, been extended beyond the narrow meaning of "speech" and "press" to include nonverbal communicative activity. It has become the practice to refer to such communicative activity as "symbolic speech." (That is an inapt phrase, of course, since speech itself is symbolic, a sound or a written figure representing an idea. A better phrase would be "nonverbal communication," though that has the undesirable characteristic of not using the precise language of the First Amendment.) "Symbolic speech" has been held to include such activities as a silent sit-in in a public library,[46] the wearing of an armband,[47] and the flying of a flag.[48] The Supreme Court has said that "we cannot accept the view that an apparently limitless variety of conduct can be labeled 'speech' whenever the person engaging in the conduct intends thereby to express an idea."[49] That has to be so, since the most unambiguous expression of personal disapproval is murder; or of disagreement with a particular law, the flouting of that law. Wherever the limits of "symbolic speech" are, however, the Supreme Court has held that they do not exclude nude dancing,[50] and my court has held that they do not exclude sleeping.[51]

In addition to "symbolic speech," the cases recognize a category of what they call "speech-plus"—verbally communicative activity closely joined with other conduct that thereby acquires, to some degree, First Amendment protection. The most prominent example is picketing.[52]

It seems clear from the cases that verbal communication forms the core of First Amendment protection and. that "symbolic speech" and "speech-plus," whatever the contours of those categories may be, are entitled to somewhat lesser protection. As the Supreme Court has put it, "the First and Fourteenth Amendments [do not] afford the same kind of freedom to those who would communicate ideas by conduct such as patrolling, marching and picketing on streets and highways as these amendments afford to those who communicate by pure speech."[53]

This list of categories is not exhaustive. But it suffices, I think, to convey some appreciation of the difficulty and complexity of a First Amendment determination. I doubt whether many would question the validity of the categories I have just described; surely the presence or absence of the various elements to which those categories pertain is highly relevant to whether, and to what extent, speech can be abridged. Imagine, then, a situation that overlaps, as many do, several different categories that have heightened and reduced protection—for example, symbolic speech about a political topic by a minor to a soldier on private property. The variations are innumerable, and if that does not make the answer difficult enough to predict, we must bear in mind that the *degree* of "heightened" or "reduced" protection that the various categories entail is entirely unspecified and inherently unspecifiable. One does not get three "plus" First Amendment points for speaking about a political subject, and two "minuses" for addressing a minor. The calculation is indeed so ineffable that it may seem more to resemble a jury determination on a matter such as whether negligence was proven than a court determination of what the Constitution requires. That is indeed what some prominent jurists have in effect acknowledged and approved. "The demands of free speech in a democratic society," said Felix Frankfurter, "are better served by candid and informed weighing of the competing interests, within the confines of the judicial process, than by announcing dogmas too inflexible for the non-Euclidean problems to be solved."[54]

Perhaps so. But one of the prime requisites for justice in any legal system is equivalent treatment of equivalent cases—or, to put it more simply, equal protection of the laws. It is not clear to me that this can be achieved through a "candid and informed weighing of the competing interests" by roughly four hundred different federal district judges, reviewed by panels of varying composition, from case to case, in twelve different circuits, and then rarely reviewed by the Supreme Court. It seems to me that a great concern with respect to First Amendment law, as with respect to other fields, is that elegant refinement may have produced a system in which perfect justice in the individual case is theoretically more likely, but equivalent justice in the whole body of cases impossible.

It is easier to state the problem than to suggest its solution. I indeed see no solution, other than unacceptable reversion to the pre–World War I regime in which virtually all restrictions on speech would be approved, or the ushering in of a new regime in which even the most basic restrictions would not be allowed. Even if we assume that the courts are free to reinterpret the First Amendment *ad libitum,* uniformity does not seem worth the cost of uniform foolishness.

The only consolation I can offer is that perhaps, in the real world, the problem of disuniformity is not as severe as theory would suggest. We lawyers, constantly dealing with the categories of legal abstractions, sometimes forget that there is really no such thing as a "First Amendment case." Lawsuits are not *about* the First Amendment, but about some concrete and fact-bound wrong that was allegedly inflicted upon the plaintiff. In the real world, it is less meaningful to talk about "First Amendment cases" than about libel suits by public figures; suits challenging the dismissal of public employees for their expression of views; suits challenging the proscription of commercial advertising on various grounds. Within these and the many other areas of what might be termed the existential categories of common First Amendment cases, there may, and I think does, develop a consistency and uniformity that cannot be expected within the category of "First Amendment law" as a whole.

NOTES

1. This essay reproduces a speech delivered at Macalester College on September 11, 1986, at which time Supreme Court Justice Scalia was a judge on the United States Court of Appeals for the District of Columbia Circuit.

2. Schenck v. United States, 249 U.S. 47 (1919).

3. "The First Amendment in Its Forgotten Years," *Yale Law Journal* 90 (1981):514–95.

4. Davis v. Massachusetts, 167 U.S. 43 (1897).

5. Gompers v. Bucks Stove & Range Co., 221 U.S. 418 (1911).

6. Mutual Film Corp. v. Industrial Commission of Ohio, 236 U.S. 230 (1915).

7. Patterson v. Colorado, 205 U.S. 454 (1907) (Holmes, J.).

8. Fox v. Washington, 236 U.S. 273 (1915) (Holmes, J.).

9. Turner v. Williams, 194 U.S. 279 (1904).

10. Robertson v. Baldwin, 165 U.S. 275, 281 (1897).

11. Patterson v. Colorado, *supra.*

12. Brief for U.S. at 46–47, Lewis Publishing Co. v. Morgan, 229 U.S. 288 (1913).

13. Rabban, "First Amendment in Its Forgotten Years," p. 540, n. 2.

14. Alexander Meiklejohn, "The First Amendment Is an Absolute," in *The Supreme Court Review: 1961,* ed. Philip B. Kurland (Chicago: Univ. of Chicago Press), 1961, pp. 245–66.

15. Lebron v. WMATA, 749 F.2d 893 (D.C. Cir. 1984).

16. Abood v. Detroit Board of Education, 431 U.S. 209, 231 (1977).

17. Miller v. California, 413 U.S. 15, 24 (1973).

18. Brandenburg v. Ohio, 395 U.S. 444, 447 (1969) (per curiam).

19. *See, e.g.,* City of Renton v. Playtime Theatres, Inc., 106 S. Ct. 925, 929 (1986); FCC v. Pacifica Foundation, 438 U.S. 726, 742–48 (1978) (plurality opinion); Young v. American Mini Theatres, Inc., 427 U.S. 50, 66 (1976) (plurality opinion).

20. Virginia State Board of Pharmacy v. Virginia Citizens Consumer Council, Inc., 425 U.S. 748, 762 (1976).

21. Posadas de Puerto Rico Associates v. Tourism Co., 106 S. Ct. 2968, 2976 (1986).

22. *See, e.g.,* Virginia Board of Pharmacy, 425 U.S. at 771–72 n.24.

23. *See, e.g.,* Pittsburgh Press Co. v. Pittsburgh Commission on Human Relations, 413 U.S. 376 (1973), which was overruled in Virginia State Board of Pharmacy, *supra.*

24. Mutual Film Corp., 236 U.S. at 243–44.

25. Gertz v. Robert Welch, Inc., 418 U.S. 323, 339–40 (1974).

26. *See* Bates v. State Bar of Arizona, 433 U.S. 350 (1977).

27. Tomei v. Finley, 512 F. Supp. 695 (N.D. Ill. 1981).

28. Brown v. Glines, 444 U.S. 348, 354 (1980) (quoting Parker v. Levy, 417 U.S. 733, 758 (1974)).

29. Erznoznik v. City of Jacksonville, 422 U.S. 205, 214 n.11 (1975) (quoting Tinker v. Des Moines School District, 393 U.S. 503, 515 (1969) (Stewart, J., concurring)).

30. Martin v. Lauer, 686 F.2d 24, 31 (D.C. Cir. 1982).

31. *See, e.g.,* Dun & Bradstreet, Inc. v. Greenmoss Builders, Inc., 472 U.S. 749, 773 (1985) (White, J., concurring); *id.* at 783–84 (Brennan, J., joined by Marshall, Blackmun, and Stevens, JJ., dissenting).

32. Bethel School District No. 403 v. Fraser, 106 S. Ct. 3159 (1986).

33. Pell v. Procunier, 417 U.S. 817, 822 (1974).

34. *See, e.g.,* Ginsberg v. New York, 390 U.S. 629 (1968) (sexually explicit material).

35. Givhan v. Western Line Consolidated School District, 439 U.S. 410, 415 (1979).

36. Erznoznik, 422 U.S. at 209.

37. Lehman v. City of Shaker Heights, 418 U.S. 298 (1974).

38. *See* Rowen v. Post Office Department, 397 U.S. 728, 736–38 (1970).

39. Southwestern Promotions, Ltd v. Conrad, 420 U.S. 546 (1975).

40. Greer v. Spock, 424 U.S. 828 (1966).

41. Hudgens v. NLRB, 424 U.S. 507 (1976).

42. Metromedia, Inc. v. City of San Diego, 453 U.S. 490, 501 (1981) (quoting Kovacs v. Cooper, 336 U.S. 77, 97 (1949) (Jackson, J., concurring)).

43. Kovacs, *supra.*

44. Miami Herald Publishing Co. v. Tornillo, 418 U.S. 241 (1974).

45. Red Lion Broadcasting Co. v. FCC, 395 U.S. 367 (1969); CBS, Inc. v. FCC, 453 U.S. 367 (1981).

46. Brown v. Louisiana, 383 U.S. 131 (1966).

47. Tinker v. Des Moines School District, 393 U.S. 503 (1969).

48. Stromberg v. California, 283 U.S. 359 (1931).

49. United States v. O'Brien, 391 U.S. 367, 376 (1968).

50. Schad v. Mount Ephraim, 452 U.S. 61, 65–66 (1980).

51. Community for Creative Non-Violence v. Watt, 703 F.2d 586 (D.C. Cir. 1983) (en banc), *rev'd on other grounds sub nom.* Clark v. Community for Creative Non-Violence, 468 U.S. 288 (1984).

52. *See* Teamsters Local 695 v. Vogt, 354 U.S. 284, 289–92 (1957).

53. Cox v. Louisiana, 379 U.S. 536, 555 (1965).

54. Dennis v. United States, 341 U.S. 494, 524–25 (1951).

2

THE NEED FOR A
NEW ENLIGHTENMENT

Lessons in Liberty from
the Eighteenth Century

Norman Dorsen

1

The relationship between the liberal arts and free expression is potentially both profound and trite. It is profound because it implicates what are, or should be, the deepest purposes of a free society. It can be trite because discussion of these purposes is often superficial, even mechanical, as we pay the expected homage to homilies we have heard from our earliest school days.

Webster defines the liberal arts as "studies (such as language, philosophy, history, literature, and abstract science) in a college or university intended to provide . . . general knowledge and to develop the general intellectual capacities (as reason and judgment) as opposed to professional or vocational skills."[1] A liberal education is said to "seek no reward beyond itself. It portends no practicality save to shape the capacities to think clearly, to express oneself precisely, and to reason humanely and creatively." It is "meant to instill a love of learning, and a love of the pursuit of learning, for its own sake."[2]

Who can object to these purposes and values as so expressed? Do they not represent the coveted realm of all educated and humane people, the Valhalla and Shangri-la of our most civilized dreams? Similarly, I have rarely found a person who openly belittles the freedom of speech. Conscious of the First Amendment—"Congress shall make no law abridging the freedom of speech, or of the press"—and the centuries of intellectual ferment and strife that gave rise to it, we enthusiastically extol the constitutional guarantee and its beneficent rewards.

But unreflective praise, whether of the liberal arts or freedom of speech, is rarely useful. Justice Oliver Wendell Holmes put the matter tersely when he wrote that "general propositions do not decide concrete cases."[3] If this were not so, our society, and others less fortunate, would not be eternally facing the question of how to connect what we learn intellectually from the liberal arts with how we live day to day, how to reconcile the majestic teachings of Western civilization with the crime, deceit, greed, and simple unfairness that surround us. At the same time, when we examine specific forms of expression, we find unresolved conflict within our society over whether to protect speech that is said to threaten our national security and sexual morality, speech that is said to offend women and racial or religious groups, and speech that is defamatory or invades personal privacy. How should we accommodate these interests with freedom of speech? Note that I have not referred to what *courts* might do in particular situations but what *society* will do. Courts and lawyers play an important role in the framing and resolution of disputes (some may feel in the *creation* of disputes also). But contrary to apparent popular belief, it is the people who decide these matters. Some years ago, Judge Learned Hand said, in a celebrated passage, that "when liberty dies in the hearts of men and women . . . no constitution, no law, no court can even do much to help it."[4] If this is true, it is the people and not the judges who ultimately must defend liberal arts and free expression.

The two concepts are mutually reinforcing. Free speech is essential to education, especially to a liberal education, which encourages the search for truths in art and science. If expression is restricted, the range of inquiry is also curtailed. This much I would hope is common ground. It is perhaps more controversial that teachers do not teach unless they take sides and express opinions, especially unpopular ones. Alexander Meiklejohn, the philosopher and libertarian, held to this view. "To be a teacher, a

leader," he says, "[one] must be going somewhere. [O]ne must
be a believer in some plan of human living."[5]

Conversely, the liberal arts gird free speech. They encourage
the development of human faculties, and, by providing exposure to a world of ideas and achievements, they encourage the
expression of new ideas. The liberal arts also encourage speech
by inducing skepticism and tolerance, which are a direct result
of the perception that human error has existed throughout human history until challenged and exposed. The courage to doubt
is the product of a world view, supported by the liberal arts, that
includes the possibility of changing the minds of others and,
often more difficult, changing one's own mind.

With these thoughts as background, I would like to turn to
some contemporary problems that engage liberal arts and free
expression, and in so doing seek helpful insights from the Enlightenment, the period of Western culture roughly embodying
the second half of the eighteenth century. In the popular mind,
this period—and its leading thinkers, such as Voltaire, Rousseau, Hume, and Kant—embodied "an emancipation of mind,
. . . a declared principle of freedom of thought, a militant ideal
of rational criticism."[6] And so it did. But that is not all it did, and
for the rest it earned the enmity of political and religious tradi-
tionalists. The Enlightenment vigorously questioned received
values, including the existence of an active god who determined
the affairs of man. New theories concerning the nature of authority and the relationship between citizen and state, combined
with growing social mobility and urbanization, weakened community ties and the power of governments. When revolution occurred in the New World and in France—and when in France it
violently uprooted so much of the old ways—the *philosophes*
whose words were thought to spark the upheaval became reso-
lutely linked with the chaos. Eventually, Napoleon and the Congress of Vienna imposed a strict but uneasy order on Western
Europe.

It is easy to forget that amidst all the political change the Enlightenment saw a vast increase in literacy—an outpouring of
words unprecedented in human history, facilitated by new print-
ing technologies, the birth of journalism, the optimistic search

for knowledge, and the investigation of nature as a living, breathing, changing, marvelous thing, displacing what for many were the sterile formulas of the received order. Nature, reason, science, and optimism were the new bywords; Alexander Pope captured them all in a verse dedicated to the Enlightenment:

> Nature and Nature's laws lay hid in the night;
> God said, Let Newton be! And all was Light.[7]

In looking to the Enlightenment for lessons I do not mean to ignore its warts. Nor was the "mind" of the period uniform, any more than was the medieval mind, although in retrospect we can see how out of diversity and raucousness came themes that gave the age a distinctive character. Still less do I want to suggest that the new learning and attitudes were born virginally in the eighteenth century. The classical tradition had its most conspicuous flowering in the West in ancient Athens, and even before that it was evident in the cultures of Egypt and China, to mention but two of the early civilizations. There, also, learning was venerated and passed on, beauty created and admired, the groundwork laid for all that followed. Closer to the eighteenth century was the great transformation caused by the Protestant Reformation and the Renaissance of the fourteenth, fifteenth, and early sixteenth centuries. Jacob Burkhardt's magnificent book *The Civilization of the Renaissance in Italy*[8] shows with unmatched learning and facility how during this period the world viewed anew the natural sciences, the beauty of landscape, the nature of individual personality, social customs, music, language, morality and religion, and, in an early use of the word, humanism. Burkhardt connects all this to antiquity, particularly early Rome, as the common source of many of the values of the Renaissance, then the modern world. This was the heritage that the Enlightenment absorbed, rearranged, deepened, and propagated.

2

Spin the reel fast forward to the waning years of the twentieth century in the United States. What are the great issues bearing on freedom of expression and the liberal arts? And what are the lessons in liberty that the Enlightenment can provide?

We enjoy a plethora of literature and art. Exciting ideas are afloat. By comparison with most, perhaps all, other countries we are blessed with much freedom, including the freedom to criticize and attack government and culture, and within limits to present daring images to the public.

But the horizon is cloudy and gray. There are too many, including powerful government officials, who deplore what they see and hear, who regard some of it as dangerous, some of it as sinful, and our liberty as license. The threats to free expression, and thus to the liberal arts, are not ghosts of the future; they surround us now. The government seeks to enjoin publication of what it regards as secrets of national security;[9] it prevents access under the Freedom of Information Act to matters of public concern;[10] it overclassifies documents that bear only a tangential relation to the national interest;[11] it prevents foreign scholars and artists from entering the United States to lecture and perform;[12] it labels certain foreign films "political propaganda";[13] it prevents Americans from traveling to certain countries;[14] it even prevents the export of American educational films that "attempt to influence opinion [or] conviction of policy . . . [or] to espouse a cause."[15] The victims of these policies are varied, although they congregate on the left end of the political spectrum. The administrations that invoke the rules also vary; Democrats and Republicans, liberals and conservatives, all have engaged in gross violations of the First Amendment.

Other forms of censorship are triggered by private groups, sometimes acting directly, sometimes through tame local governments: Generals Sharon and Westmoreland, seeking to recover vast sums from the media for alleged harm to their reputations, bring lawsuits for libel that inevitably chill free expression.[16] The heirs to Anthony Comstock seek to control the nation's reading habits by banning sexually graphic material,[17] and they are aided by some feminists who consider pornography to demean women and, without persuasive evidence, to cause sexual violence.[18] Some individuals seek to prevent peaceful demonstrations in their cities and towns because they object to the message being expressed,[19] while others remove books from the shelves of public school libraries.[20]

An especially dangerous source of censorship is the excess of religious fundamentalism, whose zealots want to lock everyone in the nation into intellectual conformity. The issue is of course not Christianity, which is rooted in the humanitarianism and altruism of the Sermon on the Mount. It is rather the zealotry and insensitivity evinced by some of its modern leaders. Thus, the Moral Majority and its allies not only want their children to pray in school, they want everyone else's to do so as well. They not only want to prevent fundamentalist women from choosing to seek an abortion, they want to deny every woman this freedom of choice.[21] They not only want their children to be taught "scientific creationism" as an alternative to science, they want every child to learn it.[22] They not only want to decide which books their children cannot read, they want to decide for everyone, even to the extent of objecting to children's stories such as Goldilocks, The Three Little Pigs, Jack and Jill, and the story of the little boy who cooks while a little girl reads to him from a cookbook.[23] (These tales are said to advance feminism and undermine Christian values.) Indeed, many fundamentalists threaten the very basis of the liberal arts by claiming that children should not be taught to question or think independently because to do so encourages them to challenge the absolute authority of God. The urge to censor is not a monopoly of any one group; the instinct is ecumenical as some Orthodox Jews, Moslem fundamentalists, and Roman Catholics plow the same furrow. The instances just noted, and many others, reveal the pervasiveness of efforts to control speech and, simultaneously, the vulnerability of free expression. With the exception of the media in the libel cases, there is no powerful constituency with an economic interest in protecting free speech. I regret to report that book publishers are not powerful (except of course in comparison to writers) and that textbook publishers often bow to the demands of special interests that seek to alter school books. It is therefore all the more necessary for each of us to do his or her utmost.

To succeed in protecting free speech, it is essential for us to understand why speech is so important to a free society, and the Enlightenment can help us—despite the prevalence of censorship in the eighteenth century. In mid-century France, even the reform magistrate of Louis XVI, M. Malesherbes, while allowing Diderot's *Encyclopédie* to be published until 1759 and other irreverent publications to appear, levied tariffs on books published abroad and rigorously controlled the number of publications in circulation.[24] In England, where prior restraints were abolished with the repeal of the licensing acts in 1695,[25] the common-law doctrine of seditious libel remained in force, permitting prosecution for "false, scandalous and malicious writing" that had "the intent to defame or to bring into contempt or disrepute" a private party or the government.[26] An accused who pleaded the truth of an utterance merely aggravated the offense; it was neither a defense to a charge nor mitigation. In the American colonies there was much censorship directed from England; and shortly after independence, in 1798, the Congress enacted the Alien and Sedition Laws, which closely tracked the English statutes.[27] The late Justice William O. Douglas graphically describes how these laws, which lasted by their terms only until 1801 and were never extended, brought a "reign of terror to the nation":

> Matthew Lyon of Vermont was fined and imprisoned for criticizing President Adams and condemning his policies toward France. Thomas Cooper was fined and imprisoned for criticizing Adams for delivering an American citizen to the British Navy for court-martial. . . . James T. Callender of Virginia was fined and imprisoned for [writing] "Take your choice, then, between Adams, war and beggary, and Jefferson, peace and competency."[28]

No, it was not the absence of censorship that marked the Enlightenment. Its hallmark was the exciting new ideas that extolled individual freedom. While the potency of these ideas waxed and waned over the years, they eventually seeped into Western thought and, whatever the lapses in practice, became assimilated into its culture and influenced the action of its governments. As Diderot, the influential editor of the *Encyclopédie*, says, "It seems to me that a being capable of feeling was intended to achieve happiness through all his thoughts. Is there any reason for setting a limit to the mind and senses and for saying to man: You shall think only thus far; you shall feel only thus far?" And Mercier writes that "[o]f all the possessions of man, thought is indisputably the most essentially undeniable. How is it possible for despotism to have conceived the project of stripping man of this faculty which constitutes his unique greatness?" [29] David Hume may have maintained that "such elemental ideas as matter, mind, and self had no clear basis in experience, and man could no more prove the uniformity of nature than the existence of God—a skepticism too radical for almost all his contemporaries." But that was not the case for Kant, who adopted as a motto for the Enlightenment *Sapere aude*, "Dare to know." Nor for the Polish general Kosciusko, a fighter in the American Revolution, who said, "As men they fought for the Holy Land, it is now for Holy Liberty that they fight." [30] Nor for Montesquieu, who observes in language anticipating Burke and Acton that "[i]t is an eternal experience that every man possessing power is tempted to abuse it." Nor for Thomas Jefferson, who said in 1787, as the new country was being formed:

> [T]he good sense of the people will always be found to be the best army. . . . The people are the only censors of their governors; and even their errors will tend to keep these to the true principles of their institutions. . . . The way to prevent irregular interpositions of [the public liberty] is to give them full information of their affairs through the channel of the public papers. [31]

The Enlightenment thinkers were also acutely aware that censorship is often the product of imposed religious conformity. They knew that Socrates had been unjustly condemned for being a cause of the attack on Athenian orthodoxy, when in fact he was merely a result. They knew of the censorship practiced by the medieval church and, after the Reformation, by Martin Luther. They knew of the religious persecution of their own day, which led so many to seek American shores in relief. While most of the eighteenth-century *philosophes* professed religious belief, and some were committed Christians, they abjured rigidity of thought, among other things using their slight knowledge of other cultures as a means of exposing the provinciality or bigotry of contemporary Christendom. Voltaire expresses the point with his customary sharpness: "Doubt is not a very agreeable state, but certainty is a ridiculous one"—ridiculous because it leads the orthodox to claim a monopoly on truth. Diderot, fearing the use of secular power for churchly ends, says, "Experience in all places and ages has proved the danger of proximity between the altar and the throne." Even the most outspoken atheist of the period, Baron d'Holbach, while maintaining that law should determine the rights of an established religion (as in Catholic France), says:

> These laws should never intrude into dogma or seek to ferret out the opinion of peaceful citizens. They will forever proscribe the intolerance, religious disputes, the harangues of fanaticism, and above all the fury of persecution. Tyranny of thought is the most cruel, revolting, and useless violation of human liberty. . . .[32]

These ideas radiated throughout Europe and reached American shores. They informed the purposes of the First Amendment to the Constitution, itself a child of the Enlightenment. It is time to identify these purposes explicitly so we can appreciate the premises of our cherished liberty.

The first purpose is individual fulfillment through self-expression, the very objective of the liberal arts. As Justice Louis Brandeis puts it, "The final end of the State [is] to make men free to develop their faculties."[33]

The second major purpose stresses the concept of democratic self-government, the "profound national commitment to the principle that debate on public issues should be uninhibited, robust, and wide open."[34] Such debate helps to maintain "the precarious balance between healthy cleavage and necessary consensus"[35] by facilitating social reform. The movements on behalf of labor unions, racial minorities, and women are the most important examples of social reform in this century.

A third and closely related purpose of free speech is its "checking value" against possible government corruption and excess, an apparently permanent part of the human condition.

A fourth major purpose is to advance knowledge and reveal truth. Justice Oliver Wendell Holmes says that the "best test of the truth is the power of the thought to get itself accepted in the competition of the market."[36] While this may seem unduly optimistic at times, the purifying quality of speech has been evident for centuries in many spheres of human endeavor, especially the arts and sciences.

Each of these purposes can be traced to the values of the Enlightenment. Taken together, they mount a powerful case for the
maximum protection of free speech. They form the basis for an
intense, not a grudging, commitment to free expression, and
through it to the liberal arts. Without this intense commitment,
the legislator, the administrator, the judge, or the scholar, after
paying the obligatory homage to free expression, will nevertheless regretfully conclude that "in *this* case" it must yield for reasons of national security, or domestic order, or government efficiency, or one of the other reasons that are regularly advanced to
overwhelm our fragile constitutional guarantee.

We must recognize that these reasons often seem powerful
and can seductively tempt policy-makers to abridge the freedom
of speech. We must recognize also that in certain cases free
speech can become too costly. All good things can be abused.
Food can gorge, drink can bloat, both can poison. Speech that
disrupts a proceeding of the U.S. Senate, that advertises a bottle
containing cyanide as aspirin, that intentionally transfers a military secret to a foreign government, or that wakes a neighbor-
hood at 4 A.M. cannot be permitted. Further, people do say foolish and vicious things, and we may suspect that their words
cause foolish and vicious acts. But to say that speculative harm
traced to language justifies restrictions on free speech is to re-
verse the value judgment made by those who wrote the First
Amendment and lived through the turbulent times that begot it.
They said, by all means punish the lawless act but protect the
freedom of speech. Even though the Congress nodded in 1798,
when it passed the Sedition Act, it soon saw the error and allowed the law to lapse. In any event, it is now clear, as the Supreme Court said in 1964, that "the attack upon the validity of
the Sedition Act . . . 'carried the day in the court of history.'" [37]
The law was not only unconstitutional but, if I may say so,
counter-Enlightenment.

The maximum-protection theory that I suggest would not ab-
solutely protect the content of all speech, but it would assure
that speech can be restricted only where an identified harm results that cannot be remedied, mitigated, or prevented by "more
speech." Again Justice Brandeis: "If there be time to expose

through discussion the falsehood and fallacies, to avert the evil
by the processes of education, the remedy to be applied is more
speech, not enforced silence."[38] While a maximum-protection
theory does not syllogistically resolve particular controversies, it
does establish the correct major premise under our Constitution, and it shows us the proper approach to many recent cases.

It shows, for example, that the Supreme Court was right in re-
jecting prior restraint on speech in the Pentagon Papers case[39]
and wrong in permitting it when Frank Snepp, a CIA agent,
wrote a book about the Vietnam War that concededly contained
no classified information.[40]

It shows that libel actions such as those brought by General
Westmoreland and General Sharon should not be tolerated, but
should be decided in the forum of public opinion as the essentially political and historical controversies that they are.

It shows that laws to restrict sexually explicit material are, in
the words of the *New York Times*, the product of "bluenosed censors" and "an unconstitutional assault on expression"[41] because
in the last analysis they would permit government to rule art.

It shows that attempts to prevent peaceful protests are inconsistent with the First Amendment, whether such protests are directed against labor organizers in the 1930s, civil-rights workers
or antiwar demonstrators in the 1960s, or gay activists, the Jewish Defense League, or American Nazis in the 1980s.

It shows, finally, that the government policy that prevents
Americans from traveling to certain countries and that bars foreign speakers from entering the United States on political grounds
is tragically wrong.

If you are tempted to question these assertions, recall the sad
list of those whose works have been censored throughout history. Galileo, Shakespeare, Mark Twain, and James Joyce are but
a representative sampling of a list that in our own day includes
Anne Frank, Bernard Malamud, and Kurt Vonnegut, among
scores of others whose works are the very essence of the liberal
arts. The censors in all these cases acted from a misguided mor-
alism, thinking that they alone knew the truth.

Bear in mind also that the question in these cases is not whether we agree with any or all of the things that were said, but whether the government should be given the power to decide what may be spoken or written. Do we really want government officials to decide what we can read and hear? The current attorney general? Any attorney general?

Hard practical considerations also support a maximum-protection approach to free speech, because the government apparatus required to enforce limitations on speech, by its very nature, tends toward administrative extremes. This is what Lord Acton meant when he said that power corrupts. Professor Tom Emerson, a foremost scholar of the First Amendment, has explained:

> Officials charged with the duties of suppression already have or tend to develop excessive zeal. . . . [The] techniques of enforcement—the investigations, surveillance, searches and seizures, secret informers—all tend to exert a repressive influence on freedom of expression. In addition, the restrictive measures are readily subject . . . to use for ulterior purposes.[42]

3

It is for all these reasons that we must cherish free expression and resist its restraint. Elimination of restrictions on speech will do much to enable our people to enjoy the blessings of liberty, political and personal, including enjoyment of the liberal arts. But there are obstacles other than the censor to the full realization of the human spirit and a just system of freedom of expression. In conclusion I shall suggest the nature of these problems and, where possible, connect them to the Enlightenment.

The first problem is the most severe: inequality. Dean Jerome Barron of George Washington University believes that current First Amendment theory is captured by a "romantic conception of free expression, a belief that the marketplace of ideas is freely accessible." The late A. J. Liebling made the point humorously when he said that "freedom of the press belongs to those who own one." Fred Friendly, professor of journalism at Columbia and former vice-president of the Ford Foundation, has commented thoughtfully on the consequences of technological change:

The drafters of the First Amendment assumed that all citizens speak with equal tongues at reasonably equal decibels. The pamphlets of Tom Paine, beyond their biting eloquence, afforded him no strong advantage over Alexander Hamilton. In turn, Hamilton wielded great power but he could not drown out the iconoclastic Paine by amplifying his own words through an exclusive bullhorn. . . . The advent of radio forever eliminated this equality, and whatever radio did to the speaker's platform, television has done to radio. . . .[43]

The healthy vision the framers of our Constitution had of a society of roughly equal yeomen has also been eroded in recent years by the conglomerate ownership of newspapers, radio and TV stations, and book publishers, as well as by the corporate veil that shrouds these companies from serious public scrutiny. What should be done? One possibility is forced access to newspapers and magazines on the part of the ordinary citizen, similar to the limited access that the so-called Fairness Doctrine permits with the electronic media, whereby the FCC enforces a semblance of balanced reporting.[44] But the Fairness Doctrine has existed for many decades, and critics like Messrs. Barron and Friendly believe that it has achieved little. More important, a guaranteed and broadened right of access to all media would inevitably require government coercion, a cure which many, including the ACLU, regard as worse than the disease. In 1974, the Supreme Court reached the same conclusion. Writing for a unanimous Court, Chief Justice Burger said,

> A responsible press is an undoubtedly desirable goal, but press responsibility is not mandated by the Constitution and like many other virtues it cannot be legislated. . . . Government-enforced right of access inescapably "dampens the vigor and limits the variety of public debate."[45]

One may heartily agree with these words, as I do, yet fear the inequality that remains. Indeed, many think it is the central problem of our society, with manifestations almost everywhere, including in the realm of free speech.

If we look to the Enlightenment for guidance, we must recall that it was far removed from our technological society and that liberty, not equality, was its central concern. African slavery was widely practiced. And while Montesquieu may have contributed greatly to political philosophy by developing the theory of separation of governmental powers, he also imposed a fierce double standard on women, deploring not only their fall from virtue but even the appearance of it.[46] Jean-Jacques Rousseau, on the other hand, somewhat anticipated contemporary concerns relating to economic inequality. While observing that all individuals need not have the same amount of power and wealth, he nevertheless asserted that "no citizen shall have so much wealth that he can buy another, and none so little that he is forced to sell himself."[47] A great challenge to the liberal arts—and to American society— in the next century will be to help us move in the direction of Rousseau's hope. This goal will not be achieved, I might observe, unless a way is found to curb the rampant greed that afflicts so much of our culture. Unfortunately, as the novelist Louis Auchincloss has said recently, "Selfishness and ruthlessness bring rewards."[48] The only hope is in our reversing this historic pattern.

A second major obstacle to a just system of free expression is intolerance. An official form of this malady is at the root of many smug government efforts to silence all opposition. But the affliction arises elsewhere. It took one form on university campuses during the Vietnam War, when opponents of the war frequently disrupted speeches by those who supported it. Heckling has a legitimate place in public discourse, but when it reaches the point that a speaker cannot be heard, it is unacceptable. Unfortunately, vestiges of this behavior apparently persist on a few campuses. A more recent example of intolerance has occurred at the hands of an organization calling itself Accuracy in Academia. This group has recruited spies—both students and outsiders— to monitor targeted professors whom they suspect of being "subversive" or "leftist." So far this effort to intimidate has been relatively limited, but we learned during the McCarthy period of the 1950s that small beginnings can lead to sinister ends. Academic freedom is a vital link in the relationship between liberal arts and free expression, and it must be jealously guarded.

I have called these two forms of behavior intolerance. They could also be called lack of self-discipline by those who, confident of their virtue, cannot bear to hear, and do not want others to hear, another viewpoint. Rousseau addressed this theme: he believed that man must discipline himself as he adjusts to the ever more complex demands of state and society. It is a form of self-discipline to protect the thought we hate when we have the power to throttle it. That is exactly what the principle underlying the First Amendment requires.

I have noted how inequality and intolerance, as well as censorship, impede the free interchange of ideas so necessary for the flourishing of the liberal arts. Another impediment is cowardice. I do not mean physical cowardice, although possibly deep-down that is involved also. I mean fear of new ideas and resulting social change, whether it is the cataclysmic change heralded by the Renaissance or the lesser but nevertheless wrenching change during this century as first Roman Catholics, then Jews, and finally blacks and immigrants from Asia and Latin America have sought a place at the high table, and as women and homosexuals have pressed for their fair share. We must understand those who fear change, even sympathize with them: free speech can sometimes lead to disorder, to challenges to personal moral codes, or to reforms that some find unwelcome.

Courage is particularly needed these days. The world is riven by ideological, national, and communal animosities. Unless we air our differences and try to reconcile them through an exchange of ideas, we abandon ourselves to those who would impose their will by force. As Anthony Lewis recently wrote for Harvard University's 350th anniversary, "Terrorism has us in its psychological grip. . . . We feel a loss of control. Order unravels. Institutions lose their self-confidence. Reason itself—the belief that human problems have rational solutions—is under attack."[49]

But the solution is not censorship, is not to view free speech as just another "value" to be jettisoned when it becomes inconvenient. A wise and principled conservative justice of the Supreme Court, the late John Marshall Harlan, recognized that "the constitutional right of free expression is powerful medicine in a society as diverse and populous as ours." But he concluded that "no other approach would comport with the premise of individual dignity and choice upon which our political system rests."[50] The Enlightenment is also instructive. Justice Brandeis wrote the following passage sixty years ago, but it could have been written in 1776.

> Those who won our independence were not cowards. They did not fear political change. They did not exalt order at the cost of liberty. [They were] courageous, self-reliant men, with confidence in the power of free and fearless reasoning applied through the processes of popular government. . . .[51]

If we are to fulfill the promise of the Constitution, there must be a tolerance of ideas and styles of expression that we despise, and at the same time, as Justice Douglas said some years ago, the encouragement of moderation and reason in advocacy and debate.

In the last analysis, it will be the values of the liberal arts—and of the Enlightenment—that will secure our freedom: Tolerance, not hate; courage, not fear. Just as the eighteenth century witnessed challenges to old ideas and the old order, we see today new challenges to established patterns of hierarchy and orthodoxy. While we must recall that not every new idea is a good idea, we also must be aware that we can never know which is which unless all are heard and tested by logic and experience. A. Bartlett Giamatti, president emeritus of Yale University, is a classicist dedicated to the liberal arts. Upon his retirement, he said:

> [T]he health of education rests on the need constantly to be mindful of the crucial distinction between education and indoctrination. There are many who lust for the simple answers of doctrine or decree. . . . They are the terrorists of the mind. Doctrine closes the mind and kills the spirit whenever it is construed as self-contained and closed, whenever it requires exclusivity of adherence or application or both, and whenever it claims to explain all that has happened to humanity or will happen.[52]

The pursuit of truth wherever it may lie is the essence of the liberal arts. As the beneficiaries of a free society and a privileged education, all of us have a duty to pursue the truth and to protect the freedom of expression that makes possible the search for a new Enlightenment. As a famous sage said in the second century, "You are not required to complete the work, but neither are you free to desist from it."[53]

NOTES

The author is grateful to Mitra Behroozi and Thomas Viles, former fellows in the Arthur Garfield Hays Civil Liberties Program at New York University Law School, for their valuable research assistance.

1. *Webster's New Collegiate Dictionary*, s.v. "liberal arts."
2. A. Bartlett Giamatti, "A Liberal Education and Residential Colleges," *Yale Weekly Bulletin and Calendar*, 6–13 Sept. 1982, p. 1.
3. Lochner v. New York, 198 U.S. 45, 76 (1905) (Holmes, J., dissenting).
4. Learned Hand, "The Spirit of Liberty," in *The Spirit of Liberty: Papers and Addresses of Learned Hand*, ed. Irving Dilliard (New York: Knopf, 1952), pp. 189, 190.
5. Alexander Meiklejohn, "Teachers and Controversial Questions," in *Alexander Meiklejohn: Teacher of Freedom*, ed. Cynthia S. Brown (Berkeley, Calif.: Meiklejohn Civil Liberties Institute, 1981), pp. 204, 209.
6. Herbert Muller, *Freedom in the Western World* (New York: Harper and Row, 1963), p. 314.
7. Pope quoted in *ibid.*, p. 315.
8. See generally Jakob Burckhardt, *The Civilization of the Renaissance in Italy*, trans. S. G. C. Middlemore (London: Harrap, 1929).
9. *See, e.g.*, Snepp v. United States, 444 U.S. 507 (1980); New York Times Co. v. United States, 403 U.S. 713 (1971).
10. *See, e.g.*, Bevis v. National Security Council, No. 85–2933 (D.D.C. filed Sept. 16, 1985).
11. *See, e.g.*, The Nation v. Haig, First Principles, July 1986, at 7 (D. Mass. 1980) (unpublished decision).
12. *See, e.g.*, Kleindienst v. Mandel, 408 U.S. 753 (1972); Harvard L. School Forum v. Schultz, 633 F. Supp. 525 (D. Mass.), *vacated*, No. 86-1371 (1st Cir. June 18, 1986); Abourezk v. Reagan, 785 F.2d 1043 (D.C. Cir.), *cert. granted*, 107 S. Ct. 666 (1986).
13. *See* Meese v. Keene, 107 S. Ct. 1862 (1987), (use of term *political propaganda* to identify materials subject to disclosure requirements of Foreign Agents Registration Act is constitutional).
14. *See, e.g.*, Regan v. Wald, 468 U.S. 222, *reh. denied*, 469 U.S. 912 (1984).
15. *See, e.g.*, Bullfrog Films v. Wick, 646 F. Supp. 492 (C.D. Cal. 1986).
16. Sharon v. Time, Inc., 599 F. Supp. 538 (S.D.N.Y. 1984); Sharon v. Time, Inc., 575 F. Supp. 1162 (S.D.N.Y. 1983); Westmoreland v. CBS, 601

F. Supp. 66 (S.D.N.Y. 1984); Westmoreland v. CBS, 596 F. Supp. 1170 (S.D.N.Y. 1984).

17. See generally Carol S. Vance, "Porn in the U.S.A.: The Meese on the Road," *Nation*, 9 Aug. 1986, p. 1.

18. *See, e.g.*, American Booksellers Ass'n, Inc. v. Hudnut, 598 F. Supp. 1316 (S.D. Ind. 1984), *aff'd*, 771 F.2d 323 (7th Cir. 1985), *aff'd mem.*, 106 S. Ct. 1172 (1986); Andrea Dworkin, *Pornography: Men Possessing Women* (New York: Putnam, 1981); Susan Griffin, *Pornography and Silence* (New York: Harper and Row, 1982); Laura Lederer, ed., *Take Back the Night: Women on Pornography* (New York: Morrow, 1980).

19. *See, e.g.*, Collin v. Smith, 578 F.2d 1197 (7th Cir.), *cert. denied*, 439 U.S. 916 (1978); Village of Skokie v. National Socialist Party of America, 51 Ill. App. 3d 279, 366 N.E.2d 347 (1977).

20. *See, e.g.*, Board of Educ., Island Trees v. Pico, 457 U.S. 853 (1982); Mozert v. Hawkins Cty. School Sys., 579 F. Supp. 1051 (D. Tenn. 1984), *rev'd*, 765 F.2d 75 (6th Cir. 1985); Grove v. Mead School Dist. No. 354, 753 F.2d 1528 (9th Cir.), *cert. denied*, 106 S. St. 85 (1985); Johnson v. Stuart, 702 F.2d 193 (9th Cir. 1983); Pratt v. Indiana School Dist., 670 F.2d 771 (8th Cir. 1982); Bicknell v. Vergennes High School Bd., 638 F.2d 438 (2d Cir. 1980); Zykan v. Warsaw Community School Bd., 631 F.2d 1300 (7th cir. 1980); Cary v. Board of Educ., Arapahoe School Dist., 598 F.2d 535 (10th Cir. 1979); Minarcini v. Strongsville City Dist., 541 F.2d 577 (6th Cir. 1976); Presidents Council v. Community School Bd. No. 25, 457 F.2d 289 (2d Cir.), *cert. denied*, 409 U.S. 998 (1972).

21. *See, e.g.*, Ari L. Goldman, Paul Weyrich, and Colin Campbell, "Catholicism, Democracy and the Case of Father Curran," *New York Times*, 24 Aug. 1986, sec. E, p. 7, col. 1; Weyrich, "Deep in Our Hearts, We're All Cultural Conservatives," commentary, *Washington Post*, national weekly edition, 19 May 1986, p. 23, col. 1; Campbell, "Church and Political Issues: How Far is Too Far?" *New York Times*, 12 May 1986, sec. A, p. 8, col. 1.

22. *See* Edwards v. Agillard, 107 S. Ct. 2573 (1987) (Louisiana law requiring the teaching of "Creation Science" violates Establishment Clause).

23. "Intolerant Zealots Threaten Our Schools," editorial, *USA Today*, 23 July 1986, sec. A, p. 8, col. 1; Beverly LaHaye, "Offensive Textbooks Threaten Our Schools," guest editorial, *USA Today*, 23 July 1986, sec. A, p. 8, col. 6.

24. See Muller, *Freedom*, p. 331 n. 7.

25. 11 H. C. Jour. 305 (1696); *see also* Near v. Minnesota, 238 U.S. 697, 713–14 (1931); Nelson B. Lasson, *The History and Development of the Fourth Amendment to the United States Constitution* (Baltimore: The Johns Hopkins Press, 1937), pp. 31–34, 37–39.

26. Act of July 14, 1798, ch. 74 § 2, 1 Stat. 596 (exp. Mar. 3, 1801).

27. *Id.*

28. William O. Douglas, "The Society of the Dialogue," in *Humanistic Education and Western Civilization*, ed. Arthur A. Cohen (New York: Holt, Rinehart and Winston, 1964), pp. 44, 48.

29. Diderot, "Observations on the Instructions of the Empress of Russia to the Deputies for the Drawing Up of Laws," in *The Age of Enlightenment*, ed. Lester G. Crocker (New York: Walker, 1969), pp. 255, 258; Louis Sébastien Mercier, "The Year 2440—A Dream If There Ever Was One" in Crocker, *The Age of Enlightenment*, pp. 247, 248.

30. See Muller, *Freedom*, pp. 319, n. 7, 320, 378.

31. Montesquieu quoted in Alfred Cobban, *In Search of Humanity: The Role of the Enlightenment in Modern History* (New York: Braziller, 1960), p. 102; Jefferson, letter to Col. Edward Carrington, 16 Jan. 1787, in vol. 6 of *The Writings of Thomas Jefferson*, ed. Andrew A. Lipscomb (Washington, D.C.: Thomas Jefferson Memorial Association, 1903–1904), pp. 55–59.

32. Voltaire and Diderot quoted in Muller, *Freedom*, pp. 335 n. 7, 255; Paul Henri Thiry, Baron d'Holbach, "Ethnocracy, or Government Founded on Morals," in Crocker, *The Age of Enlightenment*, pp. 249, 252.

33. Whitney v. California, 274 U.S. 357, 375 (1927) (Brandeis, J., concurring).

34. New York Times Co. v. Sullivan, 376 U.S. 254, 270 (1964).

35. Thomas I. Emerson, *Toward a General Theory of the First Amendment* (New York: Random House, 1966), p. 11.

36. Abrams v. United States, 250 U.S. 616, 630 (1919) (Holmes, J., dissenting).

37. New York Times Co. v. Sullivan, 376 U.S. at 276, and *id.* at 298 n.1 (Goldberg, J., concurring).

38. Whitney v. California, 274 U.S. at 377 (Brandeis, J., concurring).

39. New York Times Co. v. United States, *supra*.

40. Snepp v. United States, *supra*.

41. *New York Times*, 19 Nov. 1984, sec. A, p. 22, col. 1.

42. Thomas I. Emerson, *The System of Freedom of Expression* (New York: Random House, 1971), pp. 10–11.

43. Jerome A. Barron, "Access to the Press—A New First Amendment Right," *Harvard Law Review*, 80 (1967): 1641–78; Fred Friendly, *The Good Guys, the Bad Guys, and the First Amendment: Free Speech Vs. Fairness in Broadcasting* (New York: Random House, Vintage Books, 1977), p. 15.

44. 47 U.S.C. § 315 (1982); *see generally* Red Lion Broadcasting v. Federal Communications Comm'n, 395 U.S. 367 (1969).

45. Miami Herald Publishing Co. v. Tornillo, 418 U.S. 241, 256–57 (1974) (quoting New York Times Co. v. Sullivan, 376 U.S. at 279).

46. See Montesquieu, "Spirit of Laws," in Crocker, *The Age of Enlightenment*, pp. 182, 195.

47. Rousseau, *The Social Contract*, trans. Willmore Kendall (Lake Bluff, Ill.: Regnery-Gateway, 1954), p. 76.

48. Dinitia Smith, "The Old Master and the Yuppie," *New York*, 18 Aug. 1986, pp. 31, 32.

49. Anthony Lewis, *Harvard Magazine*, 89, no. 1 (1986), p. 147.

50. Cohen v. California, 403 U.S. 14, 24 (1971).

51. Whitney v. California, 274 U.S. at 376–77 (Brandeis, J., concurring).

52. A. Bartlett Giamatti, "Freedom of the Mind Comes First," *U.S. News and World Report*, 16 June 1986, p. 64.

53. Rabbi Tarphon quoted in Harold Bloom, Introduction to Olivier R. d'Allones, *Musical Variations on Jewish Thought*, trans. Judith Greenberg (New York: Braziller, 1984), pp. 26–27.

3

FREEDOM OF EXPRESSION AS A GENDERED PHENOMENON

Mary Beth Norton

On February 4, 1720, John Trenchard and Thomas Gordon, the "Real Whig" polemicists of early eighteenth-century England, published an important essay in their series *Cato's Letters*. (For those not familiar with recent scholarship on the American Revolution, it should be noted here that "Cato" has been identified by historians as one of the crucial influences on the formulation of the colonists' revolutionary ideology.) In this letter (No. 15), entitled "Of Freedom and Speech: That the same is inseparable from Publick Liberty," Cato puts forth the earliest-known definition of free speech that accords with our modern notions of what the concept properly entails. Trenchard and Gordon, who were harsh critics of the British government in their own day, place no limits on freedom of expression. In this they part company with their better-known predecessor John Milton, who—despite some frequently quoted rhetoric on the glories of free speech—would have denied that freedom to Catholics, reserving it exclusively for fellow Protestants.

Cato draws no such invidious distinctions. Let me quote some excerpts from this essay, in which the historian Leonard W. Levy rightly locates the origins of the ideas later embodied in the First Amendment. Cato begins by asserting, "Without Freedom of Thought, there can be no such Thing as Wisdom; and no such Thing as publick Liberty, without Freedom of Speech: Which is the Right of every Man, as far as by it he does not hurt and controul the Right of another. . . ." He goes on to declare that freedom of speech is "essential to free Government"; that it distinguishes free from repressive political regimes; that the best rulers know that free speech should be "encouraged and promoted"; that "it produces excellent Writers, and encourages Men of fine Genius"; and accordingly that "every one who loves Liberty ought to encourage Freedom of Speech."[1] Cato also explains precisely what he thinks the function of free speech is—or should be—in a particular polity:

> The Administration of Government is nothing else, but the Attendance of the Trustees of the People upon the Interest and Affairs of the People. And as it is the Part and Business of the People, for whose Sake alone all publick Matters are, or ought to be transacted, to see whether they be well or ill transacted; so it is the Interest, and ought to be the Ambition, of all honest Magistrates, to have their Deeds openly examined, and publickly scanned: Only the wicked Governors of Men dread what is said of them. . . .[2]

Thus for Cato freedom of speech is closely linked to politics. Although he declares that it would produce "excellent Writers" and "men of fine Genius," who presumably could work in any field of intellectual endeavor, he is primarily concerned with that freedom of expression that involves critics of government policy like himself. He wants to persuade magistrates that it is in their best interest to allow dissenters free rein—a task modern journalists still engage in when they manage to uncover those stories their governments would rather suppress.

Trenchard and Gordon, Cato's authors, were the product of a remarkable era of intellectual ferment that has profoundly affected the United States. That age was, of course, the Enlightenment, usually defined as encompassing the century between the English Glorious Revolution (1688–1689) and the beginning of the French Revolution in 1789. One of the Enlightenment's most systematic and insightful chroniclers, Peter Gay, begins his history of the age by observing:

> The men of the Enlightenment united on a vastly ambitious program, a program of secularism, humanity, cosmopolitanism, and freedom, above all, freedom in its many forms—freedom from arbitrary power, freedom of speech, freedom of trade, freedom to realize one's talents, freedom of aesthetic response, freedom, in a word, of moral man to make his own way in the world.

The names of those men of the Enlightenment are well known to us—the early writers like John Locke and Voltaire, the later ones like Benjamin Franklin, David Hume, Jean-Jacques Rousseau, and Thomas Jefferson—for all of them contributed to shaping our contemporary political and intellectual world. This is especially true in the United States, since the constitution that still governs us was drafted in accordance with the best principles of "enlightened" political thought.[3]

Undoubtedly some gender-conscious readers have already noticed what I now intend to point out explicitly—that is, that both Cato *and* Gay, the modern historian of Trenchard and Gordon's era, employ the words *man* and *men* to describe the participants in the freedom the Enlightenment sought. Recall Cato's ringing phrases: "Freedom of Speech: Which is the Right of every Man"; it "encourages Men of fine Genius."

But, but—I can hear someone objecting silently at this point—until very recent years *man* has been both a sex-specific *and* a generic noun in English. We have understood it, in particular contexts, to mean not the *male* of the human species, but rather all of humankind; and surely the Enlightenment theorists (and indeed their historian) were using the term in that general sense, rather than as a specific reference to males. Indeed, an attentive reader will recall that the longest passage I quoted from Cato used the terms "the People" and "publick" rather than speaking of "men." Yet in another essay Cato defines what he means by the word *Publick:* "What is the Publick," he asks, "but the collective Body of private Men?"[4] Even if the essayists did not so carefully clarify their terminology, the fact that their primary concern is politics clinches the argument that they are excluding women from consideration—for politics, everyone in the eighteenth century understood, was the proper realm of men, not women. And as for Peter Gay, the indexes to his two-volume history of the Enlightenment disclose that he fails to discuss any of the women who might have been seen as contributors to the movement he studies in such detail.

I am not alone in concluding that the *philosophes'* use of the term *man* is—as my friend Linda K. Kerber puts it—"in fact literal, not generic." The political scientist Susan Moller Okin, whose excellent work shall be referred to later, discusses this subject extensively in the introduction to her 1979 book, *Women in Western Political Thought*. "The great tradition of political philosophy," she observes, "consists, generally speaking, of writings by men, for men, and about men." Although the use of what she terms "supposedly generic" and "allegedly inclusive" words like *mankind* and *he* tends to obscure the androcentric orientation of most political thought, she notes, "we do not need to look far into [the philosophers'] writings to realize that such an assumption is unfounded." Reviewing a number of pertinent examples, she demonstrates that the term "human nature," as employed by political theorists like Aristotle, Machiavelli, Locke, Rousseau, and others, "is intended to refer only to male human nature." Her conclusion is devastating:

> Thus there has been, and continues to be, within the traditions of political philosophy and political culture, a pervasive tendency to make allegedly general statements as if the human race were not divided into two sexes, and then either to ignore the female sex altogether, or to proceed to discuss it in terms not at all consistent with the assertions that have been made about "man" and "humanity."[5]

My concern here is not, of course, political philosophy in general but rather the specific issue of freedom of expression in the liberal arts. But, since current American notions of free speech rest so firmly on Enlightenment foundations, it seems to be essential to examine in some depth the origins of our definition so as to expose its "gendered" basis. To put it briefly and bluntly: freedom of expression as the concept was formally developed in the eighteenth century applied only to men—and primarily to men acting in their political capacity. As a result, its applicability to women, not only because of their sexual identity but also because they had no formal political role, was highly problematic. If today women can be said to have obtained freedom of expression in the United States, they have achieved that goal through their own efforts, not because a "great man" of the past sought to extend them the right of free speech. Eventually, women were to take the androcentric ideals of the Enlightenment and deliberately reshape them to fit their own purposes. Just a small part of that long process will be chronicled here.

Leonard Levy has identified the three preconditions that allowed the ideal of free speech for males to gain currency in the eighteenth-century Anglo-American world. First, religious opinions had to be regarded as relative, rather than absolute, which was the long-term consequence of the Protestant sectarianism introduced by the Reformation in the sixteenth century. Second, kings and parliaments had to be stable enough to survive heated political criticism, which occurred in England as a result of the success of the Glorious Revolution late in the seventeenth century. And third, the people had to be seen as the ultimate source of political power rather than solely as its subjects, which development also followed the Glorious Revolution. Thus the Great Britain of Trenchard and Gordon's day met all Levy's criteria for fostering freedom of speech—at least political speech—among men.[6]

No one has yet asked the parallel question: what are the preconditions for freedom of expression by women? What enables women to dissent? More important, what allows them to dissent in one particular way: from their society's definition of their place in it? In short, what circumstances foster "feminist" thought, and how have women perceived those circumstances?[7]

I will pursue these questions in the following manner: after a discussion of the insights offered by the first feminist writer in the history of the world, I will turn to an analysis of two pairs of Enlightenment thinkers, one from the late seventeenth century, the other from the late eighteenth. Each pair is composed of a well-known male and a little-known female theorist. I will conclude with the first collective use of Enlightenment ideas by American women.

Who, then, deserves the title of the first feminist? Before we can confer such a title, it is essential to define the term "feminism." At a fundamental level, I would argue that a feminist must display two characteristics: first, she must recognize that women as a social group suffer certain disabilities as a result of their sex;

and second, she must advocate some sort of program to overcome those disabilities. In other words, a woman who questions her own position but does not extend that questioning to the treatment of the rest of her sex would not, under my definition, qualify for the label "feminist." (I have in mind here someone like Anne Hutchinson, who obstinately defended her right to speak publicly on religious topics, but who is not known to have generalized from her own case to that of other women.)[8]

In fact, the first feminist predated Anne Hutchinson by more than two centuries: Christine de Pizan, who was born in Venice in 1365, was the first woman (a recent translator notes) to write a work "in praise of women," one with themes that "transcend their own time." This remarkable person was the daughter of the astrologer to the court of the French king Charles V, and she was almost wholly self-educated. Married at fifteen to a twenty-four-year-old man her father had selected for her, she lived happily with her husband until his death in 1389. Since her father had predeceased her spouse, Christine at the age of twenty-five found herself solely responsible for supporting a family that included her two children, her mother, and her two younger brothers. Initiating a pattern that would characterize feminists at least through the nineteenth century, Christine—encouraged by the patronage of her family's influential noble friends and stimulated by access to their libraries—turned to her pen for subsistence. Before she died (sometime after 1429), she wrote more than twenty major works of prose and poetry and hundreds of short poems. She did not hesitate to venture where most women might fear to tread; for example, she composed a book discussing military ethics (the later editor of which chose to conceal her sex), and she boldly criticized the much-praised thirteenth-century author of the epic poem *The Romance of the Rose*, Jean de Meung. My remarks will focus on Christine's most important work on women, *The Book of the City of Ladies*, written between December 1404 and April 1405.[9]

This book begins with an extraordinary story, one that *Ms.* magazine would today term a "click" experience—that is, an incident in which a woman suddenly realizes that something she has previously taken for granted or ignored is in fact related to systematic discrimination against her sex. It seems highly likely that an event like this actually occurred in Christine de Pizan's life, for it is very vividly described, but even if the incident was a product of her imagination, that she could have such a fantasy is also revealing.

Christine tells us that one day, after she had been reading "weighty" authors in her study for a long time, she decided to relax by reading poetry. By chance she picked up a book a friend had loaned her, a volume filled with misogynistic statements. The book, Christine recounts, "made me wonder how it happened that so many different men—and learned men among them—have been and are so inclined to express both in speaking and in their treatises and writings so many wicked insults about women and their behavior." Christine measured those assessments against her knowledge of her own behavior and that of her female friends and acquaintances—a process, I might add, bearing great resemblance to the discussions that took place in feminist consciousness-raising groups in the late 1960s and early 1970s—and, she reports, "I could not see or realize how their claims could be true." Nevertheless, she argued with herself, "saying that it would be impossible that so many famous men . . . could have spoken falsely on so many occasions. . . ." She became depressed as she considered her inherent inferiority, found herself "transfixed . . . in a stupor," and cried out to God, " 'Why did You not let me be born in the world as a man? . . .' " Thus troubled, she rested her head on her chair.[10]

Christine then informs us that "a ray of light" fell on her, and that she saw "three crowned ladies" standing before her. The ladies, she later learned, were the personifications of Reason, Rectitude, and Justice, who declared they had come " 'to bring you out of the ignorance which so blinds your own intellect that you shun what you know for a certainty. . . .' " They then proceeded to instruct Christine on how to build a "City of Ladies," a defensive fortress in which virtuous women would forever remain secure from male invective.[11]

The Book of the City of the Ladies accordingly takes the form of a dialogue between Christine and her visitors: first she speaks to Reason, then Rectitude, then Justice. She asks them about calumnies men have directed at women, and they supply her with defenses against the false charges, not only responding in theoretical terms but also offering examples of women whose virtuous actions disproved the slander. To take just one example, Christine inquires of Rectitude "'whether what men claim, and what so many authors testify, is true . . . that life within the institution of marriage is filled and occupied with such great unhappiness for men because of women's faults and impetuosity, and because of their rancorous ill-humor?'" Rectitude assures her that "'women have never done what these books say'" and goes on to make this book the first to detail the problems faced by battered wives. Rectitude asks Christine to call to mind her own friends

> "who because of their husbands' harshness spend their weary lives in the bond of marriage in greater suffering than if they were slaves among the Saracens? My God! How many harsh beatings—without cause and without reason—how many injuries, how many cruelties, insults, humiliations, and outrages have so many upright women suffered. . . . And consider all the women who die of hunger and grief with a home full of children, while their husbands carouse dissolutely."

Rectitude next points out that the criticism of wives "'flies in the face of the truth,'" because "'men are masters over their wives, not the wives mistresses over their husbands, who would never allow their wives to have such authority.'" She adds that many marriages, like Christine's own, are happy; and gives a number of examples, drawn mainly from ancient history, of wives who dearly loved their husbands. The dialogue then moves on to another topic, the issue of whether women are capable of keeping secrets.[12]

Much of Christine's dialogue with Lady Reason relates to questions involving women's intellectual abilities, and the importance of the *Book of the City of Ladies* as an early work of feminist literature rests primarily on that discussion. She inquires of Reason whether God has honored women with "'the virtue of high understanding and great learning,'" because men so frequently claim that "'the mind of women can learn only a little.'" Reason responds with a classic environmentalist argument, the modern variant of which is familiar to anyone aware of the current controversy over women's native scientific and mathematical abilities: "'If it were customary to send daughters to school like sons, and if they were then taught the natural sciences, they would learn as thoroughly and understand the subtleties of all the arts and sciences as well as sons.'" Reason even goes on to explain why women do not know as much as men: "'They are not involved in many different things, but stay at home, where it is enough for them to run the household.'" The public, she points out to Christine, "'does not require them to get involved in the affairs which men are commissioned to execute,'" and so they learn little of politics or economics. In subsequent questions and answers, all replete with appropriate examples, Christine learns from Reason about women's discovery of new knowledge (not merely their ability to digest others' findings) and their many valuable contributions to world civilization.[13]

Thus in 1405 Christine de Pizan identifies the first precondition for freedom of expression by women: *education*. As she clearly understands, a woman cannot exercise her inherent powers of reason and demonstrate her intellectual equality with men without receiving an education comparable to theirs. As long as women are solely occupied with household tasks and denied access to learning, it is difficult if not impossible for them to compete intellectually with men. Having said this, though, Christine proposes no structure to institutionalize female education. Further, we must not anachronistically attribute to her other ideals enunciated by modern feminism. She explicitly acknowledges that women are and should be subordinate in marriage, that men and women have different natural roles to fulfill (she observes, for example, that women should not be lawyers), and that women are physically weaker—though she hints they may be intellectually stronger—than men.[14] In short, Christine de Pizan, despite the ardor of her defense of women and the range of her insights regarding their intellectual ability, was in the end a woman of her own time, the fifteenth century, rather than ours. It remained for her feminist successors to challenge their societies' treatment of women in more fundamental ways.

It was nearly three hundred years before another feminist theorist addressed the question of women's education, this time proposing a comprehensive scheme for its improvement. Although Christine de Pizan's *Book of the City of Ladies* had been translated and published in English in 1521, there is no evidence that Mary Astell was familiar with it. Astell was born in Newcastle in 1668 to a middle-class family with royalist sympathies. Educated by a clergyman uncle, she moved to London after her parents died while she was still in her teens. Astell never married; she lived in Chelsea, in regular contact with a group of female friends, many of them brilliant, well-educated women of noble birth. Well-known in literary and religious circles, Mary Astell wrote a number of major works on a variety of topics. The publication I shall focus on is *A Serious Proposal to the Ladies* (1694), her most important statement on women's education, but she also discusses other aspects of women's lives as well.[15]

Before considering Astell, let us look briefly at her much better-known male contemporary John Locke. Locke has been rightly celebrated ever since his own day for the originality and significance of his discussions of politics, society, and education. Although Locke was innovative when he thought about the relationship of men and the state or about the nature of early childhood education, however, his attitude toward women and the family can only be described as undeniably traditional. Women only appear in Locke's *Two Treatises of Civil Government* in two capacities: as mothers and as wives. Ancient philosophers—most notably, Plato and Aristotle—had examined the relationship of women and the state in some detail, because both believed that women (as the representatives of private, familial interests) could distract men from their primary allegiance to the *polis*.[16] In Locke's construct, though, women lack even that degree of potential influence. They never seem to be actors in their own right, except perhaps when engaged in rearing children; Locke sees them only as men's subordinates, without the capacity for acting independently. Accordingly, they make only fleeting appearances on his pages, primarily where he inserts them to score debating points on his chief target, the *Patriarcha* of Sir Robert Filmer.

Filmer's work was, of course, the ultimate defense of Stuart absolutism, contending that monarchy was based on the power of fathers to rule their children and husbands to rule their wives, as both were laid down in the Bible. Filmer, however, conveniently forgot that the crucial Commandment reads "Honor thy father *and mother*," and a good number of Locke's treatises, particularly the first, are devoted to pointing out the problems that develop with Filmer's arguments once mothers are taken into account. Thus, for example, Locke argues that even if one granted—which he does not—that parents have absolute power over the lives of their offspring, "this would give the father but a joint dominion with the mother over them; for nobody can deny but that the woman hath an equal share, if not the greater as nourishing the child a long time in her own body out of her own substance." Locke's main point is, though, that *parental* (not paternal) power ceases when the child—always a *son*, it is important to note—reaches maturity, and therefore such power cannot be analogous to political power, which is continuous through one's lifetime.[17]

In spite of Locke's praise for women in their role as mothers, in their capacity as wives he does not doubt their necessary subordination to their husbands. Locke asserts that "the first society was between man and wife," and that it was based on a "voluntary compact," with "mutual support and assistance." But, he notes, although a husband and wife have "one common concern," they have "different understandings," and so equality is not appropriate in a marriage. He concludes that, even though the power of the husband is limited, "it therefore being necessary that the last determination—i.e., the rule—should be placed somewhere, it naturally falls to the man's share, as the abler and the stronger."[18]

John Locke—and other early Enlightenment theorists—provided little help or guidance to women like Mary Astell who were interested in rethinking women's position. Indeed, Astell, a royalist, felt little sympathy for Locke, a major promoter of parliamentary power. Consequently her chief inspiration came from another strain of thought entirely, Cartesian rationalism. Descartes advocated introspection and the use of "right reason," both methods that appealed to women like Astell who lacked formal education in the classics. The aim was to use one's own experience and rigorous thought to discard custom, bias, and outdated assumptions. The Cartesian method encouraged Mary Astell to examine anew men's claims of women's inherent intellectual inferiority and to reject them as contrary to nature. Like Christine de Pizan, she advanced an environmentalist explanation for apparent feminine deficiencies in mental ability. Unlike Christine, however, Astell was highly critical of members of her own sex.[19]

Her purpose in writing *A Serious Proposal*, she declares forthrightly, is to render women "no longer . . . cheap and contemptible" and to remove the obstacles to their achievement, which were, she says, "acquired not natural." Astell accuses her female contemporaries of being frivolous slaves to fashion, of valuing men's opinions more than their own assessments of themselves, of (as she puts it) "imagin[ing] that our Souls were given us only for the service of our Bodies." She attributes these faults, though, not to women's own failings but rather to "mistakes in our Education," which, she asserts, "spreads its ill Influence thro' all our Lives." If women are prone to vice, she argues, the cause is "ignorance and a narrow Education," further encouraged by "imitation and custom."[20]

How then does she propose to improve the education of women? Like the Cartesian that she is, she advocates basing it on those "firm and immutable" qualities "Reason and Truth." Since in the course of their daily lives women had little time for reflection, being distracted by what she terms the "hurry and noise of the World" and "impertinent Amusements," she calls for the establishment of an institution that would be a "Religious Retirement," a "retreat from the World." There women could concentrate on glorifying God through regular prayer and, she declares, on "furnish[ing] our minds with a stock of solid and useful knowledge." In other words, she is outlining a seventeenth-century vision of a women's college. She calls it a "Seminary to stock the kingdom with pious and prudent Ladies."[21]

What I find particularly fascinating about Astell's *Serious Proposal* is that she declines to discuss many details of her scheme.

She does indicate that she thinks female scholars should study French philosophers (specifically naming Descartes, of course) and she remarks that musical training would be desirable. She declares that the residents themselves should decide how they will live, dress, and eat, and remarks upon her hope that they will eventually become teachers of other women. For her, establishing the principles on which a proper education should be based was far more important than detailed prescriptions.[22] In this she differed sharply from traditional male commentators on women's education. Commonly such authors laid out a curriculum in great detail, specifying not only what women should study, but also, and perhaps more importantly, what they should *not*. But Mary Astell, for all her criticisms of women, had confidence in their abilities to recognize what was in their own best interests, once their improper prior training had been exposed for the dangerous sham that it was.

Astell sums up her aim thus:

> And by that Learning which will be here afforded, and that leisure we have, to enquire after it, and to know and reflect on our own minds, we shall rescue our selves out of that Woful incogitancy we have slipt into, awaken our sleeping Powers, and make use of that reason which GOD has given us. We shall then begin to wonder at our Folly, that amongst all the pleasures we formerly pursued, we never attended to that most noble and delicious one which the chase of truth affords us.[23]

Mary Astell thus adds to Christine de Pizan's understanding of the critical importance of improving women's education the second precondition for freedom of expression for women: such education will require institutional support for serious, contemplative study by women, institutions that would parallel the monastic and collegial structures that had long freed at least some men from the demands of day-to-day routines.

Just as we must not mistake Christine de Pizan for a contemporary feminist thinker, though, we must also recognize Astell's essentially conservative outlook on women's role in general. Although she speaks of the need to teach women to take pride in themselves and to pay less attention to men's opinions of them, she nevertheless sees women's inevitable destiny as marriage and, in that marriage, necessary subordination to a husband. Women, she says, should not "usurp Authority where it is not allow'd them"; thus, they cannot (for example) expect to be members of the clergy. The aim of her seminary is to produce "a discreet and vertuous Gentlewoman [who] will make a better Wife than she whose mind is empty, tho her Purse be full." Indeed, she contends that the education she proposes would primarily help women to make better marriages; their new sense of self would prevent them from throwing themselves away on unworthy rascals.[24] Thus we must look beyond Astell for a person we can term one of the first modern feminists.

In the late eighteenth century two more theorists dealt systematically with the issue of women's education. The works of the Frenchman Jean-Jacques Rousseau have been repeatedly published and translated into many languages; those of the American woman Judith Sargent Murray have not been published in their entirety since she paid to have them privately printed in 1798. (A few scattered excerpts have, however, appeared in feminist anthologies published in the last fifteen years.) The divergent fates of their works reveal, once again, the continuing masculine domination of the world of free expression of thought.

Murray, the first American feminist, was born in Gloucester, Massachusetts, in 1751, into a prominent family of merchants. Married to a sea captain while she was still in her teens, she was widowed when her husband died in the West Indies, whence he had fled to escape his creditors. In 1786, after two years of struggling to repair her finances, she married John Murray, the founder of the Universalist movement in the United States. She began to write on the subject of women in the late 1770s but published most of her works on the topic as a series of essays in the *Massachusetts Magazine* in the early 1790s. In 1798 she collected these essays and other writings, publishing them in three volumes under the title *The Gleaner*.

The contrast between Rousseau's and Murray's prescriptions for women's education could not be sharper. Rousseau, celebrated as the prophet of freedom, sought that freedom only for males. The famous first sentence of *The Social Contract* ("Man is born free, and everywhere he is in chains") dramatically signals Rousseau's concern for recovering the natural freedom that he sees as every *man's* birthright. For Rousseau, as for Locke, the family is natural and hierarchical, the state artificial, composed of equal male participants. Locke draws the distinction because, as we have seen, he wants to deny that familial patriarchal power can be analogized to the political realm. Writing a century later, Rousseau has the opposite concern: he wants to ensure that political equality will not be extended by analogy into familial relationships. Despite their different emphases, though, both men view women only as the appendages of the male household heads who properly comprise political society.

Rousseau, unlike Locke, has a great deal to say on the subject of women's education. In *Emile,* he creates a model man—raised to be independent and self-sufficient in a corrupt world. Emile is never told what to do or not to do and is always directed to pay no attention to what others might think of him or his actions; Susan Moller Okin comments that "independence from others and their opinions is clearly the central value" in Emile's education. Lest we think that Rousseau's notions also apply to females, though, he also creates a model woman, Sophie, to be Emile's wife. Whereas Emile is raised to be independent, Sophie is raised to be *de*pendent. Rousseau argues that "woman is made to please and to be in subjection to man." Thus, he contends, Sophie's education has to be different from Emile's: "A woman's education must . . . be planned in relation to man. To be pleasing in his sight, to win his respect and love, to train him in childhood, to tend him in manhood, to counsel and console, to make his life pleasant and happy, these are the duties of women for all time, and this is what she should be taught while she is young." Although, declares Rousseau, "'what will people think' is the grave of a man's virtue," the same concern is "the throne of a woman's [virtue]" because she not only has to do right, she also has to preserve her reputation.[25]

Consequently, as Okin observes, Sophie "is educated just to the point where it is agreeable for Emile to converse with her without being in any danger of being threatened by her. . . . She is deliberately left with great gaps in her knowledge which Emile, tutor as well as lover and husband, will have the pleasure of remedying." In sharp contrast to Mary Astell, Rousseau also discourses at length on the things that women should not study, even under the tutelage of a loving husband:

> The search for abstract and speculative truths, for principles and axioms in science, for all that tends to wide generalisation, is beyond a woman's grasp; their studies should be thoroughly practical. It is their business to apply the principles discovered by men. . . . A woman's thoughts, beyond the range of her immediate duties, should be directed to the study of men, or the acquirement of that agreeable learning whose sole end is the formation of taste; for the works of genius are beyond her reach.[26]

Accordingly, just as Mary Astell could not look to the preeminent theorists of freedom in her day when she sought to create a vision of female autonomy and independence, so too Judith Sargent Murray could not find a model for expanding the education of women in the works of Rousseau, the most celebrated writer on education in her day. Instead, she had to turn for guidance, as did Christine de Pizan and Astell, to her own experience.

Like Rousseau, Murray gives her prescriptions for education in fictional form. She creates a model young woman, Margaretta Melworth, the orphaned ward of a loving couple, Mr. and Mrs. Vigillius. Margaretta's education is carefully planned by her foster mother to include training in English and French grammar, reading, writing, accounting, geography, history, astronomy, natural philosophy, drawing, literature, music, and dancing, in addition to needlework, cooking, and the other arts of housewifery. Mr. Vigillius, who narrates the story, remarks that "the liberally accomplished female," like Margaretta, "cannot fail of being distinguished"; that she will be "a pleasing and instructive companion" to men and women; that "should she . . . be arrested by adverse fortune, many resources of relief, of pleasure, of emolument, open themselves before her"; and that "she is not *necessarily* condemned to laborious efforts, or to the drudgery of that unremitted sameness, which the routine of the needle presents."[27]

Moreover, her foster parents teach Margaretta—in sharp contrast to Sophie—that "every thing in future depends upon her own exertions." Unlike Sophie, Margaretta learns to follow the rules of fashion only "as far as they square with the dictates of rectitude" and never to surrender herself unknowingly to the demands of custom. Thus when Margaretta at sixteen becomes infatuated with a fortune hunter, Sinisterus Courtland, her own good sense ultimately leads her to reject his advances and to marry instead the man her foster parents prefer. Likewise, when her marriage, which is based on "mutual esteem, mutual friendship, [and] mutual confidence" rather than on masculine independence and female subordination (as was Emile's and Sophie's) confronts hard times, Margaretta's honesty, loyalty, and intelligence save the day. By contrast, Emile's and Sophie's marriage ends badly, for she commits adultery and he then deserts her and their children. As Susan Moller Okin comments, in Rousseau's novel Sophie "has no alternative but to die, which she obligingly does, charming to the end," while Emile exults in his renewed independence.[28]

In *The Gleaner* No. 15, originally published in August 1793, Murray expresses her central criticism of the current state of women's education—and her target is precisely the practice Rousseau had advocated.

> Our girls, in general, [she observes] are bred up with one particular view, with one monopolizing consideration. . . . An establishment by marriage; this is the goal to which they are constantly pointed, the great ultimatum of every arrangement: *An old maid,* they are from infancy taught . . . [is] a contemptible being; and they have no other means of advancing themselves but in the matrimonial line.

As a result, young women, fearful of spinsterhood, accept the first man to come along, one who may not be a good choice. (Incidentally, I cannot help but think that Murray had her own youthful, unfortunate first marriage in mind when she made this point.) And so, Murray concludes,

> I would give my daughters every accomplishment which I thought proper . . . ; they should be enabled to procure for themselves the necessaries of life; independence should be placed within their grasp; and I would teach them '*to reverence themselves.*' Marriage should not be represented as their *summum bonum,* or as a certain, or even necessary, event; they should learn to respect a single life,

and even to regard it as the *most eligible*, except a warm, mutual and judicious attachment had gained the ascendancy in the bosom.[29]

Therefore Judith Sargent Murray adds to Christine de Pizan's initial recognition of the importance of education and to Mary Astell's understanding of the need for institutional support for solitude and serious, advanced study the crucial *third* precondition for freedom of expression for women: they should be educated for themselves as individuals rather than wholly as future wives and mothers. Even Mary Astell, herself a spinster, saw subordination in marriage as woman's inevitable lot. Not so Judith Sargent Murray, who stresses not only the value of egalitarian marriages but also the need for women to prepare themselves for lives on their own. Murray advocates independence for women, while Rousseau seeks it only for men. Thus Murray freed women for the first time from the confines of the traditional notion that, since girls have no alternative but to marry, they need only to learn to be housekeepers, wives, and mothers. Consequently, she laid the foundation for modern concepts of women's education, which stress the importance of developing women's talents *for their own sake*, not for the sake of future husbands or sons. She also contributed vitally to the growth of a feminist ideology that insists on seeing women *as individuals* rather than as an inextricable part of a family unit.

It was, however, the generation that followed Murray's (including Elizabeth Cady Stanton, Susan B. Anthony, and the rest of the members of the first feminist movement in the United States) who innovatively applied Enlightenment theories to women. With women conceptually—if by no means actually—freed from the restrictions of the family, notions that the eighteenth-century *philosophes* had promulgated with respect to the only fully independent persons in their society—adult white men—could be extended to encompass not only women but also blacks. And so the antebellum years witnessed the vast expansion of freedom of expression among both groups, but especially among middle-class white women, who had been the chief beneficiaries of the educational reforms that followed the American Revolution.

The Seneca Falls convention of 1848, whose "Declaration of Sentiments" deliberately mimicked the Declaration of Independence, was but the first collective public attempt on the part of American women to engage in a dialogue with men about their position in society, a dialogue that has by no means ended. I want to close by quoting some lines from the 1848 Declaration, containing not merely echoes of Thomas Jefferson, the author of its model, but also themes from Trenchard and Gordon, Christine de Pizan, Mary Astell, and Judith Sargent Murray:

> When, in the course of human events, it becomes necessary for one portion of the family of man to assume among the people of the earth a position different from that which they have hitherto occupied, but one to which the laws of nature and of nature's God entitle them, a decent respect to the opinions of mankind requires that they should declare the causes that impel them to such a course.
>
> We hold these truths to be self-evident: that all men and women are created equal. . . .
>
> The history of mankind is a history of repeated injuries and usurpations on the part of man toward woman, having in direct object the establishment of an absolute tyranny over her. . . .
>
> He has compelled her to submit to laws, in the formation of which she had no voice. . . .
>
> In the covenant of marriage, she is compelled to promise obedience to her husband, he becoming, to all intents and purposes, her master. . . .
>
> He closes against her all the avenues to wealth and distinction which he considers most honorable to himself. As a teacher of theology, medicine, or law, she is not known.
>
> He has denied her the facilities for obtaining a thorough education, all colleges being closed against her. . . .
>
> He has endeavored, in every way that he could, to destroy her confidence in her own powers, to lessen her self-respect, and to make her willing to lead a dependent and abject life. . . .
>
> We insist that [women] have immediate admission to all the rights and privileges which belong to them as citizens of the United States.[30]

In short, what Stanton and her allies were requesting was nothing more or less than the full incorporation of women into Trenchard and Gordon's "publick," the political community that fully participated in a representative government and therefore enjoyed the right of freedom of expression. Their feminism was not so much a break with the past as a logical outgrowth of it.

Insisting that the American children of the Enlightenment live up to the ambiguously general phrasing of its ideals, they used the concepts that had been forged by such pioneers as Christine de Pizan, Mary Astell, and Judith Sargent Murray to create circumstances that provided large numbers of women with the tools for exercising genuine freedom of expression. It is unlikely they will ever again be silenced.

1. David L. Jacobson, ed., *The English Libertarian Heritage: From the Writings of John Trenchard and Thomas Gordon in* The Independent Whig *and* Cato's Letters (Indianapolis, Ind.: Bobbs-Merrill, 1965), pp. 38, 40, 42, 44. This treatment of Trenchard and Gordon (and of John Milton) has been informed by the discussion in Leonard W. Levy, *Freedom of Speech and Press in Early American History: Legacy of Suppression* (New York: Harper and Row, 1963), chap. 3. On the significance of *Cato's Letters,* see in general Bernard Bailyn, *The Ideological Origins of the American Revolution* (Cambridge: Harvard Univ. Press, 1967).

2. Jacobson, *English Libertarian Heritage,* p. 39.

3. See Peter Gay, *The Enlightenment: An Interpretation,* 2 vols. (New York: Knopf, 1966, 1969). The quotation is from vol. 1, *The Rise of Modern Paganism,* p. 3.

4. Jacobson, *English Libertarian Heritage,* p. 99. On politics as the exclusive realm of men prior to the American Revolution, see Mary Beth Norton, *Liberty's Daughters: The Revolutionary Experience of American Women, 1750–1800* (Boston: Little, Brown, 1980), chap. 6.

5. Linda K. Kerber, *Women of the Republic: Intellect and Ideology in Revolutionary America* (Chapel Hill: Univ. of North Carolina Press, 1980), p. 15; Susan Moller Okin, *Women in Western Political Thought* (Princeton: Princeton Univ. Press, 1979), pp. 5, 6, 7.

6. Levy, *Freedom of Speech and Press,* p. 6.

7. Gerda Lerner, in her recent book *The Creation of Patriarchy* (New York: Oxford Univ. Press, 1986), raises some analogous issues in the introduction and chap. 11.

8. This definition resembles, but is not precisely the same as, that offered by Hilda Smith in her *Reason's Disciples: Seventeenth-Century English Feminists* (Urbana: Univ. of Illinois Press, 1982), p. 4. For an inadequate attempt to contend that Hutchinson was a feminist, see Lyle Koehler, "The Case of the American Jezebels: Anne Hutchinson and Female Agitation During the Years of Antinomian Turmoil, 1636–1640," *William and Mary Quarterly,* 3d ser., 31 (1974): 55–78.

9. Biographical information on Christine de Pizan is drawn from Angela M. Lucas, *Women in the Middle Ages: Religion, Marriage, and Letters* (New York: St. Martin's Press, 1983), pp. 138, 161–169; and Earl Jeffrey Richards's introduction to his translation of her *The Book of the City of Ladies* (New York: Persea Books, 1982), pp. xix–li (quotations from pp. xiv, xix). For another assessment of Christine's importance, see also the

foreword by Marina Warner. A popular biography is Enid McLeod, *The Order of the Rose: The Life and Ideas of Christine de Pizan* (London: Rowman and Littlefield, 1976).

10. Christine de Pizan, *Book of the City of Ladies*, pp. 3, 4, 5.

11. *Ibid.*, pp. 6–11 (quotations from p. 6).

12. *Ibid.*, pp. 117–134 (quotations from pp. 118, 119).

13. *Ibid.*, p. 63. See, in general, pp. 62–97.

14. *Ibid.*, pp. 31, 37, 63.

15. For recent discussions of Astell, see Smith, *Reason's Disciples*, pp. 117–139; and Joan K. Kinnaird, "Mary Astell: Inspired by Ideas," in *Feminist Theorists: Three Centuries of Key Women Thinkers*, ed. Dale Spender (New York: Pantheon Books, 1983), pp. 28–39.

16. See the insightful analysis in Arlene W. Saxonhouse, *Women in the History of Political Thought: Ancient Greece to Machiavelli* (New York: Praeger, 1985).

17. John Locke, *Two Treatises of Government, with a Supplement*, Patriarcha, *by Robert Filmer*, ed. Thomas I. Cook (New York: Hafner, 1947), p. 43 (I, sec. 55). See also pp. 146–59, *passim* (II, secs. 52–76).

18. *Ibid.*, pp. 159–63, *passim* (II, secs. 77, 78, 82, and 77–86). For a comparable discussion of Locke with a somewhat different emphasis, see Kerber, *Women of the Republic*, pp. 17–18.

19. On Astell's debt to Descartes, see Smith, *Reason's Disciples;* and Kinnaird, "Mary Astell," in Spender, *Feminist Theorists* (see n. 15, above).

20. Mary Astell, *A Serious Proposal to the Ladies for the Advancement of their true and greatest Interest, by a Lover of Her Sex* (London, 1694), pp. 2, 22, 25, 44.

21. *Ibid.*, pp. 47, 55, 61, 73, 75.

22. *Ibid.*, pp. 81, 88–94.

23. *Ibid.*, pp. 124–25.

24. *Ibid.*, pp. 84, 149, 154–55, 158–61. For a fuller explication of her views on marriage, see Mary Astell, *Some Reflections on Marriage* (London, 1700).

25. Okin, *Women in Western Political Thought*, p. 154 (see pp. 154–66, *passim*); Jean-Jacques Rousseau, *Emile*, trans. Barbara Foxley (London: Dent, 1957), pp. 322, 328.

26. Okin, *Women in Western Political Thought*, pp. 160–61; Rousseau, *Emile*, p. 349. Okin discusses Rousseau's works at length in part 3 of her book (pp. 97–194).

27. The story of Margaretta appears *passim* in vol. 1 of Judith Sargent Murray, *The Gleaner* (Boston, 1798). See especially essays no. 7 and 13 for the passages discussed here (quotation from p. 61). The series first appeared in the *Massachusetts Magazine* between February 1792 and December 1794.

28. Murray, *Gleaner* 1:74–75, 133. See Okin, *Women in Western Political Thought*, chap. 8, "The Fate of Rousseau's Heroines," *passim*, esp. pp. 171–72.

29. Murray, *Gleaner* 1:167–68 and 161–69, *passim*. In the *Massachusetts Magazine* of 1793, this was essay No. 15; in the compilation, it is No. 17.

30. The "Declaration" has been reprinted many times. See, e.g., Mary Jo Buhle and Paul Buhle, eds., *The Concise History of Woman Suffrage* (Urbana: Univ. of Illinois Press, 1978), pp. 94–95.

4

THE NEW PSYCHOLOGY OF HUMAN SURVIVAL

Robert Jay Lifton

Our subject is freedom of expression, and we can learn much about it from eminent experts on the law. But there are also hidden problems regarding freedom of expression that legalism cannot address. These problems involve our accessibility as ordinary citizens to certain kinds of ideas, to certain forms of consciousness. They also involve our culture's ability to impede the accessibility of information and our ability to choose. To put it plainly, there are particular issues about which we have every right to speak out, but when we try to do so, we find we lack the images and coherent thoughts to express ourselves effectively. That is because the culture throws up impediments, creating a process by which we find ourselves excluded from public discussion. Indeed, one of the greatest threats to freedom of expression that I know of is this threat of suppressed consciousness.

Such suppression creates great gaps between truly threatening external circumstances—military threats, technological threats, or social threats—and our ability to register these circumstances in our minds and to grasp them effectively in our thoughts and feelings. We become psychically numb and emotionally paralyzed, unable to think clearly in the face of terrifying reality. No subject is more suppressed in our consciousness by this psychic numbing process than the worldwide threat of nuclear destruction. Nothing, in turn, can be more subversive of the whole ideal of freedom of expression, let alone its reality, than psychic numbness.

Many factors contribute to the suppression of consciousness in the face of today's nuclear threat. Perhaps foremost among them is the mystification of the subject by nuclear strategists and decision makers, people who present themselves to us as possessors of arcane secrets and equally arcane, often deadly, visions. My aim here is to break through the numbness by describing our capacity, in Martin Buber's wonderful phrase, "to imagine the real," so that we can then begin to act on it. I want to dissolve this mystification of the nuclear threat so that we can discuss it freely and intelligently.

But to do this requires an unusual fusion of intellect and emotion, the mingling of analysis with passion. Some time ago the false idea developed in the Western tradition that thought and feeling are antagonists, that people should not let their heads be confused by the promptings of their hearts. But I know, as a physician, that brain and heart need each other desperately. Either atrophies in the absence of the other. Powerful and vigorous scholarship must always be done with passion. Passionate spiritual quests cannot be completed without intellectual rigor. And if ever an issue required the coupling of heart and mind it is the nuclear weapons issue. In the absence of this synthesis it is impossible to "imagine the real," to dissolve mystification, and to freely express oneself about the threat of global annihilation. This is what is meant by my title, "The New Psychology of Human Survival."

To begin feeling, thinking, and acting on the subject of nuclear weapons with a truly liberated consciousness requires us to confront some fundamental images. Then we must apply these images to change our outlook on a world now overloaded with nuclear weapons and with people who wish to justify them. By image I do not mean *superficial* image, such as one's personal image or the image of a particular college among high-school counselors. Instead, I refer to the primal images that direct our behavior, images that can be both individual and historical in nature. Today, I believe, our psychology is shaped by one fundamental image, the image of extinction, the image conveying the possibility that we will annihilate ourselves as a species. This image, of course, should immediately call forth its opposite, the image of denuclearization, the idea of overcoming the nuclear threat and creating a safer future. Within this dichotomy of destruction and survival imagery there are variations that alter with the times. Let me suggest quickly five sets of such images. Once these have been established the process of demystifying nuclear weapons can perhaps begin.

The first and paramount image we must confront is that of nuclear winter. Scientific studies indicate that a certain amount of megatonnage, maybe as little as one hundred megatons, exploded by anyone, will so change the earth's climate by blocking the sun with dust and debris that all human life and most other living organisms will cease to exist. Unfortunately, there is a kind of faddism built into American culture that allows people to dismiss this terrible prospect by citing contrary evidence or by dismissing scientists as not being able to come to any firm conclusions. "Well," some might say, "nuclear winter—that was last year." But nuclear winter cannot be wished away, despite scientific claims that question some of the original findings. How dead the planet might become is only a matter of degree. The larger truth is that nuclear winter epitomizes our capacity to annihilate ourselves with our own technology.

This image of total destruction should persist, and once we confront it honestly we can also see the beginnings of a new psychology that can promote our own survival. For example, there are now glimmerings of hope that the nuclear winter image is provoking an ethical shift in the consciousness of many people. As we begin to realize that any form of nuclear exchange, no matter how small, invites species suicide, we immediately begin to establish a common ethical discourse among those who embrace nuclear weapons to solve the world's problems and antinuclearists who see the diminution of nuclear stockpiles as the first requirement of survival. By recognizing the possibility of nuclear winter, both sides have begun to take the first step toward survival: dialogue with one another. This is only possible because the image itself has created a common body of knowledge about the catastrophic impact of any nuclear exchange. In short, the image of nuclear winter could offer unprecedented opportunities for the freedom of expression necessary to diminish the nuclear threat.

A second image of nuclear weapons takes us to the outermost

boundaries of what might be termed psychopathology and evil in our society. Using both words is very important because they apply to such groups as the Neo-Nazis, the Aryan Nation, and the Order, groups whose activities one sees reported on television as they practice in the hills with their heavy weapons. These people call themselves survivalists, and their plan is to welcome nuclear holocaust, live through it, and impose their nazi beliefs with force of arms on any others who remain. Though they are a fringe group, their insanely positive image of nuclear weapons is useful to antinuclearists. For when apocalyptic movements like these openly welcome nuclear devastation they certainly ratify the sanity of all people opposing the existence of such weapons. Their gleeful fantasies of seizing power after a nuclear exchange can only reinforce the truth of our own counterimage of self-genocide, add to our ability to confront it, and stiffen our resistance to neo-nazism in any form.

The third image, a contrast to nazism, is certainly more hopeful. Indeed, it is one of the most wonderful images of all associated with nuclear weapons—the Nobel Peace Prize awarded in 1985 to the International Physicians for the Prevention of Nuclear War. This symbolism has importance that far transcends the lives of those who have participated in this organization. Its largest significance derives instead from the fact that the Nobel Committee itself is not anxious to honor "fringe groups" of "fuzzy-minded intellectuals" who have vague yearnings to create a better world. Rather, the Nobel Committee's gesture expresses its recognition of the growing world hunger for truth about the nuclear threat. Its award gave symbolic recognition to our efforts to oppose the mystification and falsehood that surrounds us. And that hunger for truth represents at least the beginnings of the collective rebellion of the human mind against an uncontested journey to doomsday, a revolution against these murderous weapons and those who would use them.

The fourth image I want to present is yet another hopeful one, that of a global community united by its vulnerability. Oddly enough, it is created by the enormous increase in the danger threatened by nuclear weapons. The plain fact is that nuclear winter binds us all together, since a nuclear exchange is as dangerous to blacks in South Africa, to Chinese, and to Danes as it is to Americans or Soviets. Because the world's future is at issue, the images of worldwide interdependence and self-destruction are inspiring third-world people to take action against nuclear arms. Meanwhile, in this country we are also witnessing the growing involvement of minority groups. Even now, in New York City, several of us are forming a Center of Violence and Human Survival at the City University of New York. The Center seeks to investigate varying levels of social violence that can lead ultimately to nuclear violence. By this means all of us have begun to think in concert about *all* forms of violence, rather than one group thinking about urban violence and another group about nuclear violence. Here the new psychology of human survival is making *collaborative* freedom of expression possible. The new image of worldwide vulnerability creates the possibility of worldwide cooperation. On this issue Martin Luther King broke new ground, just as he did on so many issues. When he received his Nobel Peace Prize, he said in his acceptance speech that while he was fighting for black rights and in opposition to the Vietnam War, he also hoped to link these causes to the issue of global survival: "I refuse to accept the cynical notion that nation after nation must spiral down a militaristic stairway into the hell of nuclear destruction."

The fifth image that aids my discussion is that of the average citizen honestly questioning the technological certainty and discovering technological fallibility. Recent evidence offers every reason to do so. We need only refer to the tragic space shuttle disaster, which demonstrated on live television the fallibility of space technology, and the Chernobyl disaster, which confirmed the fallibility of nuclear technology. These failures of technology have created vivid images that increase the possibility for wisdom, for both offer serious challenges to a condition of public consciousness with roots in the 1950s that might be called nuclear normality.

Back in the Eisenhower years, the halcyon days of nuclear strategy, people like Herman Kahn made abstract, scientific-sounding assessments about nuclear weapons, leading many to believe that winning a limited nuclear war was not only possible but a wholly rational policy alternative. "Experts" making those projections presented themselves as calm and reasonable analysts. Those who protested such preparations were dismissed as emotional, unreasonable, and unscientific. Indeed, William F. Vandercook at the University of Illinois has now demonstrated conclusively that in the late fifties the U.S. government created commissions of leading social scientists and psychiatrists to develop justifications that would convince the American people to accept nuclear war—and even to behave in an orderly fashion after nuclear war had occurred.[1] Even professional circles felt the effects. Once, at a meeting of the American Psychiatric Association, which is supposed to look at psychological behavior in a reasonable way, a very gifted man named Jerome Frank began demanding that we assess the psychological dimensions of nuclear threat. Colleagues would whisper behind his back, "Hey, what's happened with Jerry? What kind of childhood trauma did he have that makes him afraid of nuclear weapons?" Now, of course, we all share his "trauma." The images of Chernobyl and the Challenger have altered our consciousness, transformed our psychology, and liberated us to begin speaking freely.

Yet the "old" consciousness continues to reassert itself, even as we struggle to establish the new. The latest excuse for "nuclear normality" comes from Harvard, the famous—or infamous—*Living with Nuclear Weapons.*[2] It is significant that the Harvard group ends its book by declaring that our only hope lies in living with nuclear weapons. The general attitude of the authors is, "Well, let's be calm about it. Don't add too many weapons that are too dangerous. Don't get rid of too many weapons. Let's just keep things balanced." It is really Herman Kahn all over again—serious, rational discussion about the "ordinary" world of nuclear weapons.

To these authors, the film satire of *Dr. Strangelove* and the antinuclear lyrics of that wonderful folk singer Tom Lehrer are simpleminded examples of atomic escapism. But from the standpoint of the new psychology of human survival Lehrer and *Dr. Strangelove* are profound expressions of sanity. When *Dr. Strangelove* ends, with a wild Texan straddling the bomb and going forth with a rebel yell before being blown into smithereens, or when Tom

Lehrer sings those wonderful lyrics "We will all go together when we go" or "So long, Mom, I'm off to drop the bomb," we are experiencing freedom of expression at its best—the utter ridicule and exposure of the absurdity of our nuclear weapons projections and the confirmation that what has been praised as reason and sanity is truly madness. Lehrer and *Strangelove*, in turn, have thus become positive images too—images of true rationality that expose the ideas of Herman Kahn and the Harvard scholars for what they are.

Nonetheless, "madness" persists in many forms, and by now we are well armed to demystify it. Take, for example, the nuclear strategy of "winning," a subject that receives great attention in the government and its hired think tanks. There, experts devise strategies for fighting and winning the war that the rest of us will most surely die in. Because of the catastrophe they are consciously orchestrating, these people keep planning for victory while simultaneously declaring that nuclear war can never be fought or won. They also project different levels, psychologically speaking, of winning. First they embrace the idea of winning in a military sense. But when reminded that such victory means global annihilation, they reply that what they *really* mean is that they wish to win the arms race by bankrupting the Soviet Union. That, of course, is one of the most common projections about the Strategic Defense Initiative (SDI). The United States, a wonderfully rich economy, will lavish so much money on SDI that the Soviet Union will bankrupt itself attempting to keep up. No one mentions the fact that the Soviet Union is just as willing as we are to win the arms race in this sense. Another claim of winning involves the so-called limited nuclear war, which of course is very unlikely to stay limited. In addition, the psychological desire for "victory" can take disastrous and false forms, such as the belief that the apocalypse of nuclear war will usher in a new "golden age." The neo-nazi survivalism referred to before is but one expression of winning survival. Certain fundamentalist groups also anticipate nuclear holocaust as a vehicle for ultimate victory. They read the predictions of Revelation and the Book of Daniel as nuclear prophesies of God's wrath and redemption. To them, victory and nuclear destruction become one and the same thing, for the destruction of the world paves the way for the second coming of Christ.

These myths of regeneration through nuclear holocaust, as I call them, can go even further into fantasy. There is for example the idea of winning by having an American, as opposed to a Soviet, Adam and Eve survive to begin the repopulation of the earth. Each of these versions of winning—limited nuclear exchanges, bankrupting the Soviet economy, welcoming Christ's second coming, or fantasizing about Adam and Eve—shows how deeply the malignant imagery and mythology of nuclear weapons has penetrated our psyches. The antidote to such destructive myths of regeneration through nuclear holocaust, is, of course, the new psychology of survival to which I have been referring, based on images of hope and truth.

Now that "winning" has been exposed for the chimera that it is, it is important to consider President Reagan's "Star Wars" program (the popular term for SDI). This program epitomizes all the concerns with winning that I have been describing. Viewed from one perspective, it seems inevitable that someone would conjure up this wild scheme, so perfectly does it epitomize governmental policies and assumptions that have held sway for decades, all based somehow on the contrary ideas that nuclear war is unthinkable but also that it is winnable. In this respect, Star Wars represents the all-inclusive fantasy of the nuclear age. At the heart of this fantasy is a radical denial of the fundamental truth of the nuclear age, that of our absolute and universal vulnerability. That is *the* nuclear truth. We are all vulnerable to these weapons, simply because of their technology. Star Wars denies this truth by offering in new form the possibility of winning. In so doing, it builds an illusion the government has fostered for decades. In *Indefensible Weapons,* a book I coauthored with Richard Falk that predicted Star Wars, I described some nuclear illusions: the illusion of limited war, the illusion that foreknowledge of enemy plans can help achieve "victory," the illusion of "preparedness" (those wonderful evacuation plans and bomb shelters the government has recommended to us), and worst of all, the illusion that stoic behavior and trust in the government will make everything turn out all right, even if there is a war![3] One way or another, Star Wars combines all these illusions, most of them decades old and enormously dangerous, into one grand illusion.

Even in the face of this grave threat, however, the new psychology of human survival has furnished us with healthy skepticism. All of the illusions have now been challenged and exposed so openly that ordinary people both here and in the Soviet Union have long ago begun to disbelieve them. Humor tells the story well because it reflects consciousness on so vivid a level. A Soviet joke, for example, has one person saying to the other, "What are our instructions, Comrade, when the nuclear air raid sirens go off?" The other replies, "You should know that, Comrade. Your instructions are to put a sheet over your head and walk very slowly to the nearest cemetery." "But," asks the first man, "why very slowly?" The second declares, "So as not to cause a panic." The humor, in this case, punctuates all illusions about preparedness, surviving, and vulnerability. Posters that have appeared in various parts of the United States offer "Instructions on behavior in a nuclear attack: Take off your glasses, open your collar, put your head between your legs, and kiss your ass goodbye." The humor, again, is folk wisdom and evidence of an undeceived consciousness. The people who make such humor understand that their governments are telling them untruths.

But officials often try to undercut these apprehensions by telling the public reassuringly cosmic falsehoods. Now we are told that the Star Wars system will protect us all from nuclear war. No more nuclear winter, no more global vulnerability. No more grim cosmic truth of total destruction. Star Wars is also presented as technology that will save us all from the errors of human decision making and therefore from the holocaust itself. Computer signals will simply record the ostensible firing of nuclear weapons, or even possible plans to do so, and then the "safety net" will automatically be activated to save us. In other words, supporters of Star Wars are trying to portray the renunciation of human responsibility as a positive good. Never mind that evidence of computer error is already all too abundant.

While Star Wars is supposed to save us by eliminating human choice, it is also supposed to do so by making nuclear weapons themselves obsolete. Strangely, however, the system actually *requires* nuclear weapons in order to release the laser beams that are to shoot down the enemy's incoming missiles. That is why the United States now says we cannot agree to the Soviet proposal to end nuclear testing. In short, our government tells us we need the testing in order to complete the nuclear component for the system that's supposed to end nuclear weapons. Of course, this is a circular argument, one that goes on forever, like all the traditional myths of "winning." Indeed, Star Wars guarantees that the arms race will continue unabated. Once the United States starts building its SDI defenses—or shields, as they are called—then even more aggressive weapons will be required to break through these shields. Such weapons, in turn, require still bigger shields, more effective defensive weapons, and so on. While promising the illusion of safety, Star Wars actually offers us nothing more than any previous arms race—that is, the *truth* of global annihilation.

Star Wars is also a crusade. It's a scientific crusade with energy and vast financial resources committed to mobilizing scientific frontiers. In these respects, it recalls the *first* technological crusade to give us victory through nuclear arms—the Manhattan Project. Old myths, it seems, die hard. The president and his allies also promote Star Wars as a moral crusade to render nuclear weapons impotent and obsolete. Indeed, the president's words, on first hearing, sound like the language that the peace movement has been using for years. But beneath the rhetoric Star Wars really revives the old image of "winning": the Soviets will be bankrupted by the SDI arms race; the United States, thanks to SDI, will be equipped to win in a nuclear war by having its own weapons and people protected by the Star Wars technology. In short, Star Wars embodies all the old themes of triumphalism, now disguised by extraordinarily complex technologies and by the language of pacifism.

Star Wars also carries powerful currents of nostalgia for that simpler time before 1945, when the people of the United States felt that they were protected from invading forces by oceans and vast distances. Those were the days before we were exposed to the nuclear truth of total destruction and universal vulnerability, and the Star Wars shield appears to promise a return to that earlier era of safety. But this view of Star Wars represents a highly manipulated perception, an intense and intentional attempt to deceive us. Psychologist Steven Kull, for example, quotes a former high-ranking Pentagon official as declaring, "The origin of SDI, that was pure perception, pure vision of the President. Somewhere in the American viscera we don't want to believe that some son of a bitch on the other side of the sky can destroy us. He's offering us that wonderful defense in the sky. It has nothing to do with military planning."[4] There is no rational basis for SDI, and the scientists working on the project know this. The new psychology of human survival requires us to recognize that deception, sometimes inadvertent and sometimes highly intentional, inspires the entire Star Wars project and that SDI embodies some of the most powerful myths our culture can generate.

Indeed, it is not excessive to state that Star Wars ultimately represents a powerful (if perverted) psychology, a problem of idolatry for theologians no less than a problem of consciousness for psychologists. For after all, what is idolatry? It is the worship of phantoms, images, false gods, the deification of forms or appearances that are visible but without substance. These objects, in turn, become objects of passionate devotion, and if ever there was idolatry, it is present in Star Wars, an idolatry imposed from the top and under false claims. As a set of idols, or as a cosmology, Star Wars promises all things to all men and women; it tantalizes their imaginations and speaks to them of safety even as it extracts enormous resources from our society. That is part of its great danger. It draws upon our scientific community; it helps undermine the availability of scientists and money for fundamental research; it plays havoc with our entire scientific economy. And as it does all these things, it also assures us that it restores America's prenuclear safety, makes victory over the Soviets inevitable, and replaces fallible human judgments with the "safety" of computers and lasers. It is this false assurance, most of all, that must be combated by people whose consciousness is informed by the truthful images of global annihilation. Those in possession of the new psychology of human survival must exercise their freedom of expression to the fullest in opposition to this idolatrous cosmology.

Perhaps the psychology of survival can best be explained by examining its opposite—the mindset of the nuclear strategists themselves. How, one wonders, can these men and women justify their work to themselves, given the terrible consequences of their creation? To answer, let me suggest a concept I developed in my study of Nazi doctors. Though nuclear strategists should not be construed as the moral equivalents of Nazi doctors, the extreme situations of work faced by both groups suggest a common principle we can learn from.

Nazi doctors came to form what I termed an "Auschwitz self," that is, a second more or less functional self that was separate from their prior selves. With this sharply divided identity, the Nazi doctor could function in Auschwitz as a killer, adapting fully to the Auschwitz environment. But outside the death camp, the other self took over, and the doctor would function in a more ordinary manner when, for instance, he visited his wife and children. Nuclear strategists, I believe, form a "nuclear weapons self" in a parallel way. One of them admitted to Stephen Kull, "Well, you have to distinguish between what you think and *what you think as a policy analyst*,"[5] implying that he was a distinctly separate person when thinking as a policy analyst instead of playing other social roles. And to compound this identity problem further there is always a great deal of "group think" in nuclear strategy circles, as Irving Janis, a psychologist, has put it.[6] People who work in the same group and who press each other toward certain positions find themselves rigorously ostracized if they deviate from the group's belief system. And, of course, the process of doubling a person's identity is enhanced by the strategists' political ideology, a belief system that polarizes pure Soviet evil against American virtue.

The greatest danger of this "doubling process" is that so many people can become involved in it, much to the peril of freedom of expression on the nuclear weapons issue. The SDI and nuclear arms programs are so pervasive, involving so many people, commanding so much political and media support at the top that societal participation is intense at all levels. In a parallel fashion societal participation in the Nazi holocaust was also pervasive. The "nuclear weapons self," like the "Auschwitz self," becomes a widespread consequence. In this respect the nuclear strategists become the primary source of larger illusion and myth that affect the whole society. Though they reflect the ideas of many other people, they should be held primarily responsible for the falsifications and illusions that fracture our sense of self and silence our dissent. Certainly, nuclear strategists and their allies possess consciences, but theirs are really *transfers* of conscience accompanying the doubling of self. In such people, as with Nazi doctors, conscience is no longer focused where it should be, on the lives or deaths of millions, or hundreds of millions, of people. Rather, the strategist thinks narrowly in terms of a vision of American survival, or in terms of getting ahead in one's particular group structure, which is furthering this kind of ideation. There is a mystical dimension involved here, a religion, if you will. The nuclear strategists see themselves as an arcane group, as the custodians of terrible and transcendent secrets. Any questioning of their work, they feel, involves fundamental challenges to their "nuclear weapons selves," that is, to their basic identities. But those of us who truly believe that we must openly confront the nuclear issue must challenge them in just this way.

In such a confrontation, what inner resources do we have? What constructive forms of self can we develop if we wish to act on the truth, to abandon nuclearism and the doubling of self? Where would our imaginations have to go? As suggested at the outset, we must embrace the truth of nuclear winter and recognize that our nuclear plight begins with global suicide. We must reach back to images of Hiroshima, devastated by what was by present standards a tiny nuclear bomb. Hiroshima became a totality of destruction, a literal nothingness. As one man, a Hiroshima physician, stated in his diary at that time, "For acres and acres the city was like a desert, except for scattered piles of brick and roof tile. I had to revise my meaning of the word destruction, or choose some other word to describe what I saw."[7] That image contains the reality of nuclear destruction, not the fantasies of Star Wars or the projections of nuclear strategists of a million killed here and a hundred million there. Another survivor also captured the essence of complete obliteration: "I climbed Hijiama Hill in the suburbs and looked down. I saw that Hiroshima had disappeared. I was shocked by the sight. I saw many things after that, but I simply cannot express what I felt. I could see Koi, a suburb and a building station, but Hiroshima just didn't exist." Again, nothingness. And that same man suggested that the proper way to commemorate the destruction of Hiroshima was to "take an area round the hyper-center where the bomb actually fell, this central place where the bomb hit, and let there just be nothing there, then close all the doors of private homes and stores in Hiroshima, let those who come find a city of the dead, and then the visitor will see that such a weapon has the power to make everything into nothing." [8]

That is the power of nuclear holocaust. But that is also an image of power that can help us form a constructive sense of self with which to combat the forces of nuclearism. Ordinarily "nothingness" suggests the spiritual disciplines of Zen Buddhism or various forms of Jewish and Christian mysticism. But the pursuit of nothingness as suggested by Hiroshima is a radically different form of spiritual regeneration. In the case of nuclear weapons "nothing" is not an abstraction or inner condition. It is literally nothingness, the end of everything forever. For this reason it is terribly difficult for our minds to move into that terrifying terrain. Nonetheless, its contours can be suggested. They are suggested in a picture on the cover of a book of essays of the International Physicians Anti-Nuclear Movement,[9] a famous picture taken by Bernard Hoffman soon after the bomb at Hiroshima. At the edge of the picture is a single cyclist with a bicycle. The rest of the picture is simply debris, an area in which houses clearly stood before. It is an overwhelming image because it conveys that sense of nothingness. A different sort of nothingness may be found at Auschwitz, where there are many exhibits. One is simply a room full of shoes, mostly baby shoes. To look upon those shoes forces the mind to do the terrible work of imagining the missing people. Again, nothingness. Nothingness in this sense can serve us in the way of imaginative wisdom. It's a starting point, a way to combat the "doubling" of self and to recognize illusion, myth, and misrepresentation for what they are.

Truly, all of us struggle with the polarities that cripple our ability to speak freely. We all lead double lives. On the one hand, we know that everything can be annihilated, everyone we've ever touched or loved, at any second. On the other hand, we go about business as usual, as though no such danger existed, and perhaps we have to, but perhaps also at a cost. Still, the threatening image of nothingness has begun to reshape our sense of self. In the last decade or so there has clearly been more of an opening of self, an honest recognition of the actual danger. As many different studies have recently begun to show, people now recognize the danger. The possibility of nothingness conflicts with the yearning for a world that is rid of nuclear stockpiles. In short, there is increasing psychological legitimacy in acknowledging nuclear fear, a new psychology of human survival.

There is also increasing recognition of the pragmatic truth of humanity's shared fate. Shared fate means very simply, "If I die, you die; if I survive, you survive." Like the recognition of nothingness, the profound truth of shared fate is transforming our sense of self, creating the beginnings of what might be called a "species self." Because of the terror that nuclear technology has imposed on us, we recognize the principle of shared fate. At this point our sense of self becomes increasingly bound up with the sense of self of everybody else in the world. The process is truly a complete reversal of the "doubling" of self among nuclear researchers. We still have our distinct personal identities: We are Americans or Russians, husbands or wives, fathers or mothers, and so forth. But if we take our species selves seriously, then every act we perform is informed by some sense of that universality of fate and therefore recognizes the need to be concerned with human rights as well as nuclear danger.

Of course this sense of species identity provides no politics or religion for eliminating the nuclear threat by any organizational means. It does not replace the necessary risks of moral and political struggles and difficult actions. It does not banish a single nuclear weapon or solve a single international dispute. But at the same time it does infuse us with a special kind of possibility and hope, derived from a new sense of self. Moreover, this sense of possibility and hope is enormously enhanced if we then take every opportunity to express ourselves freely and fully, demanding nuclear weapons disarmament. The new psychology of human survival demands nothing less than a recognition of the species self in all of us.

NOTES

1. William F. Vandercook, "Making the Very Best of the Very Worst: The 'Human Effects of Nuclear Weapons' Report of 1956," *International Security* 11 (Summer 1986): 184–95.

2. The Harvard Nuclear Study Group, *Living with Nuclear Weapons* (Cambridge: Harvard Univ. Press, 1983).

3. Robert J. Lifton and Richard Falk, *Indefensible Weapons: The Political and Psychological Case Against Nuclearism* (New York: Basic Books, 1982).

4. Steven Kull, "The Mind-Sets of Defense Policy Makers," *Psychohistory Review* 14 (Spring 1986): 28.

5. Kull, "Mind-Sets," p. 23.

6. Irving Janis, *Victims of Groupthink: A Psychological Study of Foreign Policy Decisions and Fiascoes* (Boston, Mass.: Houghton Mifflin, 1972).

7. Quoted in Robert Jay Lifton, *Death in Life: Survivors of Hiroshima* (New York: Random House, 1967; reprint, New York: Basic Books, 1982), p. 27.

8. M. Hachiya, *Hiroshima Diary* (Chapel Hill: Univ. of North Carolina Press, 1955), pp. 54–55.

9. Robert Jay Lifton, Eric Chivian, Susanna Chivian, and John E. Mack, eds. *Last Aid: The Medical Dimensions of Nuclear War* (Redding, Conn.: Freeman Press, 1982.)

5

THE CHEMISTRY REVOLUTION AND THE MEDIA

Freedom and Responsibility

Harry B. Gray

This occasion gives me an opportunity to discuss some of the most difficult trends in chemistry today and some of the most difficult problems facing the public in learning about what's going on in science. There is a revolution now in progress in chemistry that is completely reshaping every aspect of the field. And to the media, this revolution often means "big news." But "big news" too often results in headlines and stories that badly miseducate the American public about the true significance of today's scientific research. In other words, the chemists' "freedom of expression" through research has created great opportunities to address some of society's most pressing issues. The media's freedom of expression through reporting about chemistry has created thorny problems by creating false impressions in the public mind. First, let me try to describe some of the revolutionary features of chemistry research today. Then, I will relate them to the problem of public awareness, as created through the media.

Chemistry has certainly changed in the sixty years since physicists invented quantum mechanics and pronounced that "now all of chemistry is solved." While such a remark remains a source of considerable amusement to the thousands of chemists who are at work in laboratories around the world, there is, today, a persuasive case for this point of view. The revolution I just referred to does, indeed, promise that in the next few decades chemistry *will* be put on a rational basis, for we are no longer the same kinds of scientists we were in the 1940s, 50s, and 60s.

Back then, chemistry was a field where researchers mixed things together and hoped for the best. But now, that method (one I like to call "shake and bake" chemistry) is old science. Three very strong influences have made that method obsolete, while driving the chemistry revolution forward. These are (1) the reliance on theoretical chemistry, done with computers, (2) the use of lasers in chemistry research, and (3) the development of a host of new technologies that allow chemists to design and synthesize the molecules they wish. Briefly, let me describe each of these.

First, there is the computer, which makes theoretical chemistry very useful. High-speed computers can calculate the structures of molecules and also their reaction pathways. On a theoretical level, chemists now can predict much more about molecular structure and behavior than they could even ten years ago.

Second, there are lasers. Lasers have received much attention in the press, owing to the president's "Star Wars" program. But their truly constructive and less publicized significance lies in chemistry research. They allow us to examine chemical reactions that occur very rapidly, reactions that only take billionths or even *trillionths* of seconds. Thanks to lasers, it is now possible literally to see the very first events of chemical reactions, the very first movements of atoms as they separate from molecules. The understanding that lasers have provided chemists is truly phenomenal.

Third, advances in synthesis technology now allow chemists to make molecules to order. This is a development that has eliminated traditional forms of research forever. In the 1960s, chemists would walk into the laboratory and begin puttering around. They would examine some references in books and journals and begin mixing things, hoping for publishable results. Now, entering the laboratory, they head not to the bookshelf or the laboratory bench but to the computer, with its graphics screen. There in an instant the screen displays gorgeous, multicolor, three-dimensional simulations of big molecules. Since chemists already know the structures and properties of many of these molecules, they can begin manipulating them as they wish. They can command the computer to insert new atoms or to remove existing atoms. They can change a carbon into a nitrogen, an oxygen to a boron, or change whole groups of atoms, if that is what the problem calls for. And after changing the entire molecular architecture at will, the chances are good that they can go back into the lab and actually *create* the substances they have modeled on the computer.

This, in brief, is what the chemistry revolution is all about. Scientists can make the new molecules they design thanks to theory (revealed through computers), thanks to lasers that measure reactions in exquisite detail, and thanks to other new instrumentation that allows us to determine the structures of even highly complex compounds with relative ease. But strange as it may seem, few know that this great revolution has occurred. Some chemists don't even realize it, because it already has spread so broadly throughout the scientific community. And further, the media have not given the public an accurate idea of these developments or their broader social importance. I can assure you, however, that a chemistry revolution has happened.

To be more specific (following Thomas Kuhn), the revolution represents a paradigm change in chemistry. The old experimental, trial-and-error paradigm has been replaced by the "designer" paradigm. It is obvious that the power to manipulate matter almost at will has enormous implications for public policy. For this reason, chemists need to take their work far more seriously than ever before, and we must make sure that the public has a good understanding of what we are doing. That, in turn, makes our relationships with the media of primary importance and involves us all in basic questions concerning freedom of expression and *accuracy* of expression. Unfortunately, in my opinion, the nature of scientific investigation has not prepared us well, as chemists, to think about these questions.

As scientists, we have always felt that we have exercised freedom of expression, and for good reason. That is what the proper experimental method is all about. We are free, in the laboratory, to search for empirical truth. When we discover error or falsehood, we wipe it out. So experience has taught us that science and freedom of expression go together very easily. But with freedom now come new responsibilities for chemists, thanks to the changes in chemistry I've described and the enormous power that we chemists now have. Our first responsibility is, above all, to be frank and accurate in explaining what we do and what it means, hoping that the media will report it accurately. After I explain further how monumental the possibilities are, perhaps the reasons for "telling it like it is" will become self-evident.

Since, as already noted, chemists have become molecular engineers, we now can design and synthesize whole new classes of biologically active molecules. This ability means all sorts of new medical breakthroughs and advances in our struggles to increase food production. Chemists also are becoming ever more important in the production and conversion of energy. A recent example is the quest for a high-temperature superconductor. Such a material would be able to transmit large amounts of energy over long distances with unprecedented efficiency. Besides being worth trillions of dollars, such a conductor would revolutionize every aspect of the world's energy business.

Another area where chemists are front and center is the search for molecular memory. Today, all high-speed computers are based on solid-state devices such as silicon chips. But chemists know there is a much better memory, a chemically based one in which information is stored at the atomic level in molecules. Richard Feynman has examined this possibility and has suggested that molecular memory will allow us to increase the speed of today's "super computers" a million-fold or even more. Now *that's* revolutionary, and reason enough to heed the assertion that chemists bear watching in the public arena.

Today chemists are strategically placed to contribute to the five most important areas that concern the public at large: energy, materials, health, food, and environment. Without being overly dramatic, one can say with assurance that the everyday work of chemists now impinges on the health and well-being of everyone. And for this reason, we chemists have an enormous responsibility to explain our work accurately to the media and to make sure, if at all possible, that the media report our work accurately to the public. Like every other form of freedom of expression, freedom of expression in the sciences does not mean freedom from responsibility.

To explore this matter further, let me tell you about an area of my own work, my research in energy. Although you may not be aware of it, we are all facing today an energy crisis that is much more serious than the one that made so many headlines a few years ago. How can such a crisis exist when gasoline sells for under a dollar a gallon? The answer is that Americans think that because there is a temporary glut in oil there is a long-term abundance of energy. We believe all is well, even as we use up precious oil reserves at an ever-increasing rate. I can virtually guarantee that in a few years there will be another oil crisis—a giant oil crisis. In the next twenty years, we will shift abruptly from an energy system based on crude oil to an energy system based on the next great raw material that is readily available—natural gas. Chemists know this and are doing a tremendous amount of research in order to facilitate this conversion. Natural gas must be manipulated chemically in order to make drugs, materials, and fertilizers on the one hand and liquid fuels on the other.

How much has the general public heard about this impending transformation? Or even more to the point, how much does the public know about the *long-term* transformation in the energy field that chemistry must achieve by the next century? Sometime in the twenty-first century, our natural gas reserves will disappear, just as oil reserves are dwindling now. An important future source of energy could be water and sunlight, if ways could be found to use the sunlight to split water into its constituent elements, hydrogen and oxygen. Hydrogen production from water is now a glamorous field of energy research, and the media love to report on it. The field is called artificial photosynthesis: it aims to achieve, with a system synthesized by chemists, what sunlight and green plants do in nature—split water into hydrogen and oxygen. It would be an ecologically perfect process, splitting an extraordinarily available raw material (water) into a high-energy fuel (hydrogen) and nature's oxidizing agent (oxygen). Recombining the hydrogen and oxygen would create energy for running the planet, just as the natural process of photosynthesis has always done, because for billions of years it has led to the oil, coal, and natural gas we still depend on today.

Like nature, artificial photosynthesis creates no pollutants. One simply splits water into hydrogen and oxygen, using sunlight as the primary energy source, then extracts the chemical energy from the hydrogen, turning it once more into water. A perfect cycle. Indeed, what could be more perfect?

The bad news is that chemists will need at least fifteen or twenty years of further research before it will be possible to evaluate the potential of artificial photosynthesis. At the present time there are two promising approaches to the problem. The first is to emulate Mother Nature. When we take a green leaf and examine each of its three components and their working relationships, we see that component one, chlorophyll, receives sunlight; component two, a group of complicated molecules, relays electrons; and component three, an assembly of enzyme catalysts, makes oxygen and carbohydrates. At this third point, the chemist can step in and change the process so that instead of carbohydrates, hydrogen and oxygen are produced.

The second approach, my approach actually, is to build a better leaf than God's original. This takes nerve, but the research group I work with certainly has enough of that. When God built the original leaf, he gave it a particular architecture because he obviously wanted to do more than split water. Our approach, by contrast, is to start from scratch, use inorganic chemistry, and along with help from computers begin building molecules that interact as we want them to with water and sunlight. In theory, we and others have succeeded in doing this. But in practice, our work has an extraordinarily long way to go.

Sad to say, no one has yet come remotely close to building an artificial photosynthetic system that can function for more than a few cycles. The durability of our best systems falls far short of Mother Nature's, and our design flaws will take decades to correct. So while the media have helped us forget that we are now in the midst of an oil-based energy crisis, they should not be allowed to mislead us into thinking that the huge breakthroughs in chemistry I've described are leading us rapidly to an unlimited supply of environmentally clean power. Here is where freedom of expression becomes very pertinent. Here also is where we must confront the thorny problems that arise when scientists and the media interact.

Scientists need to "tell it like it is," that is, to be totally accurate when reporting publicly on their work's significance. Yet scientists also have an abiding desire to see their work reported on the "Today Show" or written up in *Business Week*. Reporters of science are no different. They know that dramatic headlines and stories capture the public's attention. Yet serious science reporters also want to make their stories accurate, interesting, understandable accounts of truly significant developments. On both sides popularity and accuracy begin to compete with each other, and here's where the problem with freedom of expression starts. Let me illustrate what I mean by offering further examples of news reporting on the subject of hydrogen energy.

The first example is dull—the totally responsible way of reporting. It involves a scientist who knows exactly what the limitations of his or her research are, is clear about long-term research goals, and is willing to work patiently with a reporter to present the story faithfully. It also involves a reporter who values accurate science stories more than sensational news. The trouble is that there are very few examples of this sort. More often than not, good science is very poorly represented in the media because it is tremendously oversold.

An example that illustrates the overselling of science comes from *Business Week*. It reports the excellent work of two distinguished groups of scientists: one from the Royal Institution, the other from the National Bureau of Standards. These two groups have made a considerable breakthrough in making fuel from water, but the headline announces much more. It reads, "Closing in on an Inexhaustible Energy Source." The story that follows goes on to state: "Now scientists are closing in on what sounds almost like a form of perpetual motion, that mimics the ability of green plants to split water." It further asserts that "scientists have developed an artificial form of chlorophyll that improves on Mother Nature's own."[1]

Unfortunately, that's just not true. In reality, Mother Nature's green leaf produces several thousand molecules of oxygen and carbohydrates before its machinery wears out. And when it starts to wear down, another system is made to replace it. In other words, nature's system is continually replenished by elegant synthetic steps. Scientists, by contrast, construct devices that wear out in *three* cycles, not three thousand. We've hardly "improved on Mother Nature's own" system, as *Business Week* claims. In fact, we have not come even remotely close to simulating Mother Nature's system.

The *Business Week* article leaves the public with a false sense of security about future energy sources. The article also fails to emphasize the real advances these experimenters have achieved. The scientists are cast in a bad light. The *Business Week* science writer has failed to give them proper credit for their breakthrough. Instead, scientific colleagues, people who know the truth, will conclude either that the scientists in question manipulate the media or that the media manipulate them. The scientists, in turn, will become understandably upset. In the future, they will not want to discuss their work with reporters, who have proven their ability to make good scientists look undeservedly foolish. Scientists will refuse to talk to the press. Freedom of expression will be stifled. The public will remain ignorant of the energy crisis we face and of scientists' efforts to deal with it.

My next case concerns the reporting of scientific claims that have yet to be proven valid, the sort of work that cannot be evaluated until it has been published and presented at a scientific conference. Nonetheless, such work often makes headlines, as for instance the headline that introduced a large article in a recent *New York Times:* "New Way Reported to Take Hydrogen from Water."[2] In this case a scientist has given a telephone interview on his unpublished work. No one knows whether or not his experiments are really valid. Moreover, he must refuse to discuss his work very specifically, since his patent attorney has advised him not to specify the metals he used in the experiments. Suddenly, unproven science had been converted into "fact" by a

New York Times headline. Next, there is a follow-up story in *Newsweek*. But when knowledgeable scientists are polled, most greet these claims with deep skepticism.

Reports of this sort do real damage. They mislead the public by presenting unproven experiments as facts. They encourage scientists to grab headlines for untested results rather than testing their work and then reporting it carefully. The *Los Angeles Times* also published an article about the case I just mentioned, rightly calling it an example of "Scientific Publication by Press Conference."[3] Whenever scientists and news reporters collaborate to advertise unproven science, as they did in this case, both freedom of expression and responsibility of expression suffer accordingly. The public learns nothing. Responsible scientists have yet another good reason for avoiding the media. Their less responsible colleagues get rewarded with headlines for work that has yet to prove its value.

Finally, let me cite a humorous example that I call "Sam Leach's box." Though this example involves outright fraud dressed up to look like science, it also makes a serious point about freedom of expression. What was Sam Leach's box? According to Patrick McDonald, vice-president of MGM Hydrotech of Los Angeles, "It is the greatest thing since sex. There will be no reason to strip mine for coal, no reason to run supertankers full of oil or build nuclear power plants."[4] That's certainly an attention getter!

In this box, Sam Leach claimed, water is split into hydrogen. Into one end Leach would pump steam. Out the other end would come a big jet of hydrogen that could be ignited, like a tremendous flame thrower. Sam Leach obtained a patent on this box, despite the obvious fact that his claims for his invention violated at least two laws of thermodynamics. Scientists know that energy is required in order to split water and that one must put energy into such a system in order to get energy out later. To the contrary, Sam Leach claimed, the water goes in, the catalyst splits it, and hydrogen comes out—forever.

All serious scientists scoffed. But, significantly, the media did not kill the story. Leach's patents began to pay off. He sold millions of dollars worth of stock in his company as investors speculated that he really had invented a perpetual motion machine. Though serious scientists were struggling to produce the smallest amounts of hydrogen from water, using sunlight, Sam Leach was making millions on an apparatus that supposedly supplied inexhaustible amounts of hydrogen from water. You can imagine my frame of mind when ABC News in Los Angeles finally did interview me to get my opinion on the box.

Of course I told the reporter, "It's impossible. The box is preposterous," and tried to explain why. But the reporter clearly wasn't interested in my scientific facts. Instead, *he* began defending Leach's box, and I kept explaining why the whole idea was absurd. Though I hung up in frustration, the reporter kept calling back. Finally, after one last accurate scientific explanation that the reporter refused to listen to, I exclaimed in frustration: "Look, I don't know everything. Maybe this guy Sam Leach knows something I *don't* know!"

As you might suspect, that statement was the only part of my long interview that made the ABC newscast. The anchorman stated solemnly: "I have been trying to get to the bottom of this story for two weeks. As you know, all the scientists I've contacted have expressed great skepticism about this box, except one. But he is Harry Gray, of the California Institute of Technology, an expert on hydrogen. After he had expressed some initial reservations, I explained the process to him. He then responded, and I quote, 'Who knows, maybe this guy Sam Leach knows something I *don't* know!'"

In that brief moment, before a vast audience of viewers, the media had made me out to be a defender of scientific fraud! Despite my careful explanation of why his box could not possibly work, ABC had made me into Leach's accomplice. My attempt to report science accurately had failed utterly, and every possible problem of the relationship between the scientist and the media had been highlighted. The entire significance and promise of chemistry's revolutionary new paradigm had been obliterated. Instead, scientists had been exploited and the public cheated.

Scientists have an obligation to the public. The public needs to be far more knowledgeable than it is now about what scientists are doing and about the pervasive social impact of research. The media have a responsibility to report scientific news accurately. It will require collaboration and hard work both by scientists and reporters to improve science reporting. But we need to begin now, because science is moving ahead ever faster. As it does, its impact on everyday life will become greater and greater.

NOTES

1. "Closing In on an Inexhaustible Energy Source," *Business Week*, 4 Aug. 1986, p. 58.

2. Walter Sullivan, "New Way Reported to Take Hydrogen from Water," *New York Times*, 8 Oct. 1982, sec. A, p. 12.

3. Lee Dembart, "Scientific Publication by Press Conference," *Los Angeles Times*, 8 Oct. 1982, sec. A, p. 1.

4. Tom Nicholson and Janet Huck, "Sam Leach's Box," *Newsweek*, 19 Apr. 1976, p. 78.

6

TALKING IN TONGUES

The Writer and the State

John Edgar Wideman

This is a conference whose official subjects are the Constitution, freedom of expression, and the liberal arts. Which means that I have license to talk about anything under the sun. One constraint I do feel, however, is the rather intimidating presence of my fellow invited guests. I consider their impressive credentials and ask myself why I am here. What news can I bring about the Constitution? Clearly I shouldn't attempt to compete with Judge Scalia or Mr. Dorsen. I'm who I am, and that's certainly not a legal scholar. Nor do I pretend to be a historian of the Constitution. I know something about those matters. I care about those matters, but I'm not going to address myself directly to them, posing as an objective, learned critic. I'm a fiction writer. Part of what I'll do here is simply tell a few stories and through this process of naming, of pointing out a series of concrete particulars, perhaps I can work outward towards the larger ideas and themes that underlie this conference. This whole business is about freedom of expression, right? So I can do it my way, right? It's a free country, isn't it?

Yesterday afternoon, a Macalester faculty member introduced

Author's Note: My talk at Macalester was orally performed rather than written. Since different aesthetics inform speaking and writing, any attempt to put my oral presentation on paper would involve not simply editing, but translating—pitch, rhythm, intensity, stage directions, and so forth. The finished product might resemble the talk, but would be a separate creation. Hence my dilemma and the compromise that follows: neither speech nor writing, the voice without a face or body, the ghost of the body imprisoned in words on the page.

me to a man from Austin, Minnesota. Suddenly I was reminded, Hey, here you are again in Minnesota—and here's that strike again. (Last spring I flew into Minnesota with Reverend Jesse Jackson's party, as Jackson attempted to initiate a healing dialogue between warring workers and owners of the Hormel meat packing plant in Austin.) The faculty member was wearing a red and white button that symbolized something like "Stop Hormel." I'm sure you know about the strike in Austin, because we're in Minnesota, and nearby is a town that's beset by a crisis. A town in which a traditional way of life—working for the company—is coming apart. That's one way of talking about it. We might also say that it's a town where chaos is loose. Two versions of reality are clashing, and one has the economic power to enforce its version of reality upon the other. A battered and beleaguered group of your fellow citizens is in deep trouble, is resisting the Hormel Company's version of reality. At great cost, workers are perpetuating a set of values, are holding themselves at odds with the most powerful institution in their community. They are demonstrating great courage, and through intense self-scrutiny they have begun to understand themselves and their struggle in terms that transcend a union-versus-management conflict. Civil rights, human rights, the power of self-determination and self-realization are issues the strikers have identified in their grievances against Hormel (issues that drew Jesse Jackson's attention to Austin). The striking workers have been aided by Macalester people, but I'm not here to applaud those acts or discuss the merits of the strike. I don't know that much about it, except that I've been in Minnesota before—in an Austin jail, in Union Halls, in the board room at Hormel—so when I saw that button, lots of things clicked into place for me.

What does all this have to do with freedom of expression? I'm not going to fill in the blanks, but I hope you keep asking yourself that question. You're going to have to help me make connections and jumps. My fiction demands conspiracy, or at least cooperation from the reader, and today I'll ask for the same sort of active participation from you.

Anyway, the man from Austin was not wearing a button. That seems strange, doesn't it? A faculty member sympathetic with the strike sports a button, but the man who is actually one of the strikers doesn't. Why? I wanted to know, so I asked. And I found out that if the worker from Austin wore a button, he could have been put in jail, jailed because a judge had issued an injunction against wearing that button. Why? I guess because somebody has the power to enforce his version of reality upon this man and restrict him. Why doesn't the button count as a form of free speech protected by the Constitution? Why is a silent button silenced? Another Macalester faculty member talked about silence and how silence fits into this whole business of freedom of expression. How voices not heard are eloquent in their absence, how their unrecorded *no* breaks through the drone of consensus. We're in Minnesota and certain folks can't wear buttons.

When I was invited to speak here, I was asked early on to send a text of my speech and then asked again, and then asked again, and finally the request became more modest. I was asked simply for the title of my speech. Now I'm a reasonable person, so somewhere about August I called up and said, "I have a title for you: 'Talking in Tongues: The Writer and the State.'" Now I thought I was being pretty clever; my title was just about as broad as the theme of the conference. I could get away with saying anything when the time for saying it arrived. Besides procrastination, I had another motive in choosing my title. I gave myself license to rise to the podium and shout: "Heenemah! Honana! Holayolayolayo . . ." You didn't understand a word of that, did you? Nonsense syllables, gibberish, babble. Probably so . . . but maybe not. Maybe I was practicing what I'm preaching about, talking in tongues.

When people are visited by the spirit of godhead, that spirit communicates in a language often unintelligible to those of us inhabiting the ordinary plane of existence. When a spirit speaks through a human vessel, both the medium and the message are wrapped in mystery. The performance must be translated in order to be understood. Only through various kinds of regimens and disciplines—both physical and mental—does someone earn the power to speak for a god. Such ideas are old, probably as old as culture. There have always been people who profess to speak for spirits, for powers, for supernatural beings larger than life, who control life. When godhead speaks it's mysterious, it's scary, and the human body expressing that speech tends to take on extraordinary powers. It glows. Holy men jump up and down for hours, chant endlessly, beat drums, go without food or rest, for days suffer incredible mortifications of the flesh. People can change their identity in front of your eyes when they are energized by this godhead. Most societies have an instrumentality, a way of conceptualizing this concept. Talking in tongues is a universal phenomenon, a way of bringing us in touch with those powers that are larger than human. This is true in traditional African religions, and one version of the idea was carried to the New World by slaves in the form of worship popularly known as voodoo. When voodoo adepts speak, they're being ridden, mounted by the ancestors, and the ancients use these people as vehicles for speaking the truth, for sharing the wisdom of the past. In the Catholic church, which may be a little more familiar, one of the tests for sainthood has to do with glossolalia, this ability to speak in tongues.

Now one irony of speaking in tongues is that most human beings don't understand what is uttered. They hear noise, babble. Stop and consider the etymology of words like *babble, barbarous,* and *barbarian.* How they demonstrate the use of language as a criterion for drawing the circle of civilization. Those who speak as we do are inside, those who don't, outside. Barbarians are people who can only babble, who don't have a language. Like barbarians, speakers with the gift of tongues are outsiders whose very existence poses a threat to the status quo. They are intruders, bringing messages we often would rather not hear. Messages that challenge our assumptions about who we are, messages couched in terms that call into question the legitimacy of the language we employ to define ourselves.

Though we are living at the fag end of the twentieth century— a chaotic century that has shattered most traditional values—we Americans profess to value reason and logic and conceive of ourselves as living under the rule of law, embodied in a constitution that protects freedom of expression. This democratic culture encourages the liberal arts. So at first glance a rather barbaric idea such as this notion of speaking in tongues doesn't have very much to do with the way we live or how we perceive ourselves today. Yet one of the jobs a writer does is to speak in tongues. A really good writer must speak in tongues because he or she brings news from *over there*, a version of events, a version of reality that literally didn't exist until the words for it were discovered, created, born.

I'm talking now about great art. I'm not talking about Muzak. I'm not talking about the soaps. I'm not talking about the novels you buy in the airport. In fact, that kind of mimicry, that kind of reproduction of our lives does not extend our lives, does not surprise us. It does just the opposite, works the other side of the street. The mass media present us with images of ourselves that are very, very familiar. And that's why they're attractive. Because they don't demand anything. A romance we read may be set in Bali or in the Himalayas; it can unfold in Dallas among the rich or in Timbuktu. Setting is irrelevant, at most the trimming for a package that rarely contains surprises. Everybody will speak our language, share our values. Exotic trimmings are fine to get the story started. Then soon, usually very soon, you find out there's a good guy, a bad guy, a beautiful woman, and the story's all about middle-class courtship and marriage. It's all about a soft lady being rescued by a hard knight and taken off happily ever after to live in suburbia.

That's the mirror this literature brings to us. It's our lives, what we choose to believe about ourselves told over and over again. Even the TV news is packaged in such a way as to remove shock, horror, surprise. First comes a pretty face, and then we hear someone who talks exactly the way we talk or think we talk. All the things that are happening across the world, across the globe, all the chaos is reduced into a kind of smilingly delivered pablum, which reminds us that we're not participants in the world. We're simply spectators, sitting in our living rooms, and what's demanded of us is not confrontation with a flood in China or with crack on the streets of Harlem. All that's being presented is homogenized into a kind of entertainment, and in this way the media transform the citizen into a spectator rather than a participant in the world. The language of the popular media works to level, reduce, and defuse—and thus performs the opposite function of art. The true artist, the artist who labors at his or her craft, is about the business of expanding our notion of reality, creating hard, crisp edges you can't swallow without a gulp.

There is a great American novel called *Invisible Man*, by Ralph Ellison, and somewhere in that book is an outcry: "Why all this rush towards conformity?" The first time I read the book that question sort of got buried because I was so excited by so much else that was going on. But as I've read and taught the novel subsequently, I've come to believe that question is the heart of the book: Why all this rush for conformity?

Another related theme in the book, an idea that you just can't swallow and walk away from is that within any pattern of certainties, chaos lives. Do you understand what that means? Perhaps I can give you an example with a joke I know. A man takes his son to the museum. This is one of those chances for fathers and sons to hang out, and the dad can incidentally pass on the heritage of Western civilization to the kid, who usually seems to be more interested in bubble gum, his walkman, and baseball cards. But the old man's going to persevere, take this kid to the museum and show him some great art. They arrive in front of a gory painting of lions and Christians in the Roman Coliseum, and the lions are definitely having more fun. There's blood all over the place, and Christians cringing, Christians jumping, Christians being devoured. As he stares, transfixed by the huge canvas, the son begins to weep, and the father thinks, "Ah, this is working, my kid's picking it up, great art is wonderful for educating the soul." So he pats his son on the head and says, "Don't cry, Son, it's OK, everything is going to work out all right. This is a terrible scene, but the Christians will triumph in the end. Even the dead ones get to be martyrs and go to heaven." The kid wipes a tear away and answers, "I wasn't crying about the Christians. There's a little baby lion in the corner, and he ain't gettin' none."

Yes, chaos lives within the pattern of all our certainties. I listened to Judge Scalia talk about freedom of expression from the point of view of the Constitution. I learned an awful lot about law and history and logic, and I enjoyed his presentation, its precision, its concreteness. Except when it was all over, I had a question: What about the robes? Yes, I understand this business of reason, logic, and precedent. But what about the robes? Why do these guys wear robes? I mean, if you're going to be logical, if you're going to use reason, and that's the justification for making a determination, for deciding this is free speech and this is protected and that is not, why do you have to wear a robe? And why do judges have to be on raised platforms? Why do they have to look down at lawyers and alleged perpetrators? And it came to me quite clearly that the law isn't simply a matter of logic and reason. The legal system also talks in tongues. Law appeals to our "primitive," visceral side as much as it attempts to convince through logic and reason.

Let me expand just a bit. Art and education both should aid us in deconstructing reality. One might say that's a fundamental gift the great artist can bestow on society. The great French writer Proust paid the ultimate compliment to Renoir, by noting that before Renoir painted them, there were no Renoir women in Paris, but afterward, you could find such women all over the streets of Paris. Proust went on to compare what the great artist does to the work of an oculist. After the oculist finishes a successful treatment, the patient's vision is transformed. Books, paintings, music, sculpture embody new ways of seeing. Great art comes as a shock to us. It disturbs our certainties, teaching us that chaos resides within them.

This suit I'm wearing, this occasion, the language I'm using, it's all part of a game we play, and the rules are arbitrary; they're rules we can follow or ignore, yet we follow either course at our peril. The rules of the game are not ordained outside of ourselves. Our history, the clothes you are wearing, the car you drive, the reason you've turned up here this morning at Macalester College, the reason you see a black man when you look up at this stage, all these things are contingent. This city, country, continent, green earth, stars, galaxies, infinities enfolding infinities, all these things, this sense we have of reality, is constructed. We make a crucial, sometimes fatal, error when we treat as given those things that we can refashion and remake and reconstruct.

People talking about law in a way that conceals the chaos within their certainties can be quite dangerous. Here I am speaking to you this morning. I'm a writer. I have a good job. I can support my family. I have access to this platform from which I speak to you. Little more than a hundred years ago my great-great-grandfather was a slave with almost none of the legal rights I enjoy. There was a Constitution then, there's a Constitution now. So what does that mean? One might argue that the Constitution is a living document, and that my circumstances, my freedoms today, simply illustrate the glory of the Constitution, its flexibility, how it can be responsive to challenges. Look at this black man. He can do things that he couldn't do twenty years ago, a hundred years ago. So we say "hurrah." But if you look a little more closely, you remember the chaos never goes away. A man in this audience from Austin can't wear a button. You look a little more closely and you realize that there are still whole classes of people not protected by the Constitution, and you remember that whatever your vision of the world is, there is somebody who is looking at it from a lower position, a different position, and the world doesn't look to that person the way it looks to you. And when you get right down to it, the world looks quite different to any two people sitting side by side. As it should. Unless someone usurps the power to say it shouldn't.

The Constitution is about power. Its history reveals wise and foolish exercises of power. The Constitution can be regarded as simply a tool of those who are in power, who control the army, the economy, who run the businesses. We can view the Constitution cynically as a now-you-see-it, now-you-don't sham, an instrument that is only used to protect certain people's rights and interests. (Where, for example, was the Constitution during World War II, when Japanese-American citizens were forced into concentration camps?) Sometimes this is a society of law and sometimes a society that isn't run by the rule of law. Sometimes you count as a human being under the Constitution, sometimes you count as two-fifths of a human being, and sometimes you don't count at all.

The scary part is how delicate that balance is. From day to day what's important, what we cherish is not a given but a precarious kind of historical accident, and what we take for granted certainly can be taken away. I suggest that perhaps one way to experience how close we are to the edge is to look at the experience of those people who are outside, to listen to those voices who seem to be speaking in tongues. What are the messages? Is the taking of a drug, is the crack epidemic, speech? Is it communication? Rather than simply throw up our hands and rant about evil and devils and try to get votes by promising to squash that epidemic, are we willing to look at deviance as a form of speech? What is the message contained in crime, delinquency, difference? And what does that message mean for us? How does it change our language, how does it change the way we see ourselves? Those are the kinds of questions art—good art—can force us to ask about ourselves. Those are the questions true artists ask about themselves.

Then I think of those robes again, those robes that are part of justice. I still don't fully understand what they mean. But there's chaos underneath those robes. There's chaos, there's a primitive side of man that law appeals to. And there is a disguise involved, the disguise of brutal power.

When the robes are donned by a judge, when we rise in respect as his or her honor enters the courtroom, we are part of a play, a drama, a performance. We're pretending that the judge is somehow in touch with transcendent powers, and we can call those law, justice, what-goes-round-comes-round, whatever. What must not be lost sight of are the stakes of the game that's being played, and how our assent sanctions and perpetuates the game. If we choose to speak the language of the courtroom or assent to it by our silence, we are approving the language of the judge, empowering the voice that can condemn us. And it's a language worth our lives and our deaths. Once the judge dons the robe and we join in the performance, we're part of the performance; we grant it license and say we'll follow along to where this performance leads. We'll believe in it, we'll take the leap, we'll decide that this version of reality is one that we want to attend to. Now maybe that's a good idea, maybe we should. And maybe the rule of law has something at its core that is a sort of salvation, that can direct us in a very confusing and treacherous world. I'm not saying that it doesn't. I'm saying that we must also continually defrock, deconstruct, understand the performance, understand the arbitrariness of it, understand that it doesn't have to be that way.

Lots of us have heard the story about the emperor and his new clothes. The emperor goes out into public supposedly wearing his wonderful, glorious suit of light. He's naked, of course, but everybody's so frightened of the emperor that nobody points out his nakedness. All the good citizens sit on the sidelines oohing and ahing about how beautiful the clothes are. I think in a strange way we have that story all backwards—at least the way it's told in our society. I'm talking about the part when a little kid pops out of the crowd and says, "Hey, that guy doesn't have any clothes on." And everybody laughs and the whole illusion passes. In that version of the story the kid's a hero. The emperor is laughed out of existence. But in fact what usually happens is the kid says, "Hey, that guy doesn't have any clothes on," and the cops come out and beat his head. Or his mother grabs him by the neck and says, "Shut up!" Then his friends don't talk to him any more because he's taken a chance, he's poked his finger through the curtain, he's reminded everybody that there's chaos beneath their pattern of uncertainties.

I've been reading a fascinating study of mental illness. *The Man Who Mistook His Wife for a Hat*, by Oliver Sacks, is a wise, funny, moving book, and Sacks describes patients who are very strange indeed. I mean if you're at a psychiatrist's office and on the way out you try to grab your wife and put her on your head because you think she's a hat, you have a serious problem. Nonetheless, Sacks emphasizes that, as far as some folks have gone awry, they are still human beings trying to cope, and there are capacities, structures within human beings that can respond to trauma and miraculously compensate. If your eyes go, your hearing becomes more acute. And that dynamic within human beings that allows us to repair ourselves is a cause for rejoicing, a cause for hope.

The bad news, though, is that so much we take for granted can go wrong. Capacities healthy people never even consider can be lost and profoundly alter the quality of life. We walk upright and balance ourselves in space, yet this most basic aptitude depends upon a fragile harmony of receptors and balancing mechanisms. I may speak in tongues, I may get confused sometimes, but my proprioceptive sense is OK—I'm vaguely perpendicular to the floor. But think a moment. Haven't you seen people who go through life bent at a strange angle because their proprioceptive sense—depending as it does on those vestibules, canals, and channels at the thresholds of the body that keep it upright—is failing?

It may be instructive to imagine the possibility that such an illness could threaten a whole society. Our mechanisms for keeping ourselves ethically and morally upright have atrophied. We're in trouble. We lean precariously to one side. We're tilted toward consensus, conformity, majority rule. We allow the majority to dictate the kind of life we may lead. We are systematically eroding and ignoring those chances we have to adjust the angle of our stance, our vision. Voices telling us we're crooked do so at their peril. Considering the Constitution in this context, I ask how real, how substantial, how protected are the rights of minorities. Are we striving to iron out a compromise between collective and individual prerogatives, or are we drifting, listing farther and farther away from the notion of the sanctity of an individual life?

Ponder the history of black people in this country—their relationship to the Constitution, their relationship to freedom of expression—and you'll find a very checkered past indeed. That history embraces us all. We've inherited a legal system, values, and institutions that for four hundred years denied the reality and personhood of twenty million black people. But push the issue of majority versus minority in another direction, one which perhaps impinges more directly on your self-interest because, finally, each of us is a minority of one. If black people as a group can be treated as outsiders, what are your chances of a hearing if your life-style is at odds with those of most other people? Whose rights went up in smoke when the MOVE people were bombed in Philadelphia? Why are we eroding the line between child and adult offenders, between treatment and punishment? Why are there more prisons and longer sentences? Are we seeking law and order or are we afraid of our children, afraid they won't be us?

Let me give a warning. When this county starts to go bonkers, when this leaning, this tilting begins to get worse, the first people to experience the reality of that tilt, to suffer its oppressive weight, will be the prison population. I have a brother who is a prisoner, and in the last few years I have watched Constitutional protections being stripped away from him and his fellow prisoners. We have a history of experimenting with the powerless. Drugs and diseases, for example, are tried out on prisoners (and economic reform begins at the bottom with welfare mothers instead of at the top with corporate raiders and inside traders). We experiment on people who are powerless, who are in many ways slaves of the state, because they have no recourse if the experiments turn harmful. After prisoners, the next group we test is children. Yesterday, prisoners' cells could be searched and trashed with impunity; today, school lockers are subject to the same treatment. If we watch passively as the rights of certain groups of outsiders are abridged, before we know it these categories of vulnerability grow broader and broader and everyone's rights disappear. It will happen step by step. According to law.

I'd like to give you a small parting story or legend that epitomizes the tilting I'm talking about and one way of dealing with the truth. The Pythagorean brotherhood in ancient Greece believed that the world in all its splendor and variety could be understood as a harmonious expression of certain mathematical relationships, that reality corresponded systematically to numbers. They extrapolated a great philosophy on that idea. Then some Pythagoreans discovered irrational numbers. The symmetry between numbers and reality was fractured. The brotherhood reacted to this discovery of irrational numbers (Greek *eretos*, "unsayable") by keeping them a secret: "Our view of the world doesn't work anymore, so let's not talk about these things, let's just forget about them." And they fomented a legend among themselves that the members of the brotherhood who discovered these irrational numbers were all lost in a shipwreck as a kind of punishment. (And what better punishment for people who discover the irrational than to be forever lost in the sea, which moves and changes and has no shape, no form?) But one of the Pythagoreans went public, and I don't know whether or not he was an artist but he should have been. He revealed the existence of irrationals. He said the unsayable. Legend has it that he was crucified by his brothers.

So to try to say what is unsayable, to take the chance of speaking out, means that maybe you're speaking in tongues. It also means that you may not be granted the protection of the Constitution. Judge Scalia pointed out that symbolic speech often falls outside the window of protection guaranteed by the First Amendment. And certainly talking in tongues, the babble of the outsider, is symbolic speech. Nobody knows what you're talking about. The noises minorities make are not even recognized as a language. But there *is* a message, there *is* substance, and if we're going to right our society, if we're going to have a chance to live as individuals, we have to remind ourselves that the price is speaking out, taking chances, and learning to make sense of the unsayable.

NOTES ON CONTRIBUTORS

Warren E. Burger recently retired as Chief Justice of the United States to chair the Commission on the Bicentennial of the United States Constitution. Known for his thoughtful and independent-minded legal conservatism, Burger led the Supreme Court during one of its most productive and influential periods. During his tenure, the Court issued landmark decisions that will continue for decades to shape legal procedure and social policy. Burger is an honorary trustee of Macalester College. As chairman of the commission leading the commemoration of the Constitution's two-hundredth anniversary, he has done much to put the Constitution in the forefront of the nation's concerns for 1987.

Norman Dorsen is one of the nation's most distinguished scholar/activists in civil liberties law. He is Stokes Professor of Law and Director of the Arthur Garfield Hays Civil Liberties Program at the New York University Law School. He served as an assistant to Joseph Welch during the U.S. Army–Joseph McCarthy hearings; since 1976, he has been president of the American Civil Liberties Union. He has argued landmark legal cases before the U.S. Supreme Court, involving such issues as the right of juveniles to due process in delinquency hearings, the constitutional rights of illegitimate children, and the rights of women to secure abortions. He is author of six major books on constitutional law and civil liberties.

Harry B. Gray recently received the National Medal of Science for research in bioinorganic and inorganic photochemistry that could lead to direct production of energy-rich molecules from sunlight. This is the latest of many awards; Gray has also received the Toleman Medal, the American Chemistry Society Award for Inorganic Chemistry, the Harrison Howe Award, and more. Gray is Arnold O. Beckman Professor of Chemistry at Gates and Crellin Laboratories, California Institute of Technology. He has published fifteen books and monographs and more than three hundred papers. A Phi Beta Kappa Scholar who has been recognized for excellence as a teacher, Gray has consulted extensively with the U.S. government and private industry.

Robert Jay Lifton is Distinguished Professor of Psychiatry and Psychology at the City University of New York—both at the John Jay College of Criminal Justice and at the Graduate School and University Center—and the Mount Sinai Medical Center. He has written widely on the relationship between individual psychology and historical change and helped form the new field of psychohistory. Lifton has written or edited fifteen books; his writings have appeared in a variety of journals on such topics as Nazi doctors and genocide, the impact of nuclear weapons on death symbolism, and the Vietnam war experience. His *Death in Life: Survivors of Hiroshima* received the National Book Award. He is a longtime leader of Physicians for Social Responsibility.

Mary Beth Norton, Professor of History at Cornell University, is widely respected as a leading scholar in the history of American women. Her most recent book, *Liberty's Daughters: The Revolutionary Experience of American Women, 1750–1800*, was judged by the *Los Angeles Times* as "simultaneously painful and delightful to read." Her first book, *The British Americans: Loyalist Exiles in England, 1774–1789*, was honored by the Society of American Historians. She has published in many journals, co-edited a collection of articles, and collaborated on a leading textbook. She delivered the 1986 Commonwealth Lecture at University College, London, and has been a prominent speaker on contemporary issues.

Antonin Scalia is widely considered one of the nation's most powerful legal thinkers. A former professor of law at Georgetown University whose nomination as associate justice of the Supreme Court was before the Senate at the time of the Wallace Conference, Scalia has developed a reputation as much for his independence of mind as for his legal conservatism. Serving in the Nixon administration, he joined the Justice Department in the midst of the Watergate crisis, taking the legal position that the famous tapes belonged to the president and not to Congress. Scalia has argued in favor of narrowing the scope of the Freedom of Information Act, defended the powers of the presidency, and dissented against broad application of the First Amendment in libel cases.

James Brewer Stewart is James Wallace Professor of History and Provost at Macalester College. The author of three major works dealing with the American antislavery movement and the coming of the Civil War, Stewart has also published fifteen articles and numerous book reviews. His most recent book is *Wendell Phillips, Liberty's Hero*.

John Edgar Wideman, one of America's foremost creative writers, has been hailed by the *Los Angeles Times Book Review* as "the black Faulkner, the soft-cover Shakespeare." His novel *Sent For You Yesterday* was selected for the prestigious P.E.N./Faulkner Award, and his family memoir, *Brothers and Keepers*, won him international acclaim and a feature spot on CBS's "60 Minutes." His most recent novel is *Reuben*. Professor of English at the University of Massachusetts, Wideman is author of many short stories and poems and has written articles for a variety of periodicals on subjects ranging from fashion to basketball. A former Rhodes Scholar, Wideman has spoken extensively throughout Europe and the Near East.